Committee on the College Student
Group for the Advancement of Psychiatry

Helping Students Adapt to Graduate School: Making the Grade

Helping Students Adapt to Graduate School: Making the Grade has been co-published simultaneously as *Journal of College Student Psychotherapy*, Volume 12, Number 2 1999.

Pre-Publication
REVIEWS,
COMMENTARIES,
EVALUATIONS . . .

"**T**he pressures of graduate school produce such enormous strains and demands on the average student that he or she feels the need either to confide in a professor or to flee from needed help. I do hope that Dr. Silber's exceptional work will be read by professors and administrators and by the students themselves. It is not a crime to need help or to speak to a professional who can provide practical assistance. Dr. Silber explains the need and a possible remedy."

Marvin Kalb
Director
Edward R. Murrow
Professor of Press and Public Policy
Harvard University
John F. Kennedy School
of Government
Cambridge, MA

D1714027

"**H**elping Students Adapt to *Graduate School: Making the Grade* breaks new ground by giving professors and students a guide to the graduate school experience. I was pleasantly surprised by the readibility of this collective effort by the Group for the Advancement of Psychiatry, Committee on the College Student. Psychiatrists sometimes have a hard time communicating clearly in writing; in this case more is better. This book is thoughtful and clear in both description and prescription; it will benefit both students and their advisors. Those concerned about the quality of graduate student life should by all means review the contents.

I was especially pleased by the ability of the authors to lay out a rationale for providing support (chapter 3) and the subsequent illustrations especially those dealing with developmental issues (Chapter 4) and Psychiatric Disorders (Chapter 7).

Graduate students are often able to understand more clearly and quickly what is going on with them. A resource such as *Helping Students Adapt to Graduate School: Making the Grade* can help immeasureably by placing their concerns in context while offering reasoned insights and solutions. Administrators will find the whole graduate school experience covered with helpful material on older students, international students and matters of gender and race. This is a very readable and helpful resource; it is a fine contribution to the literature on student life."

Dr. Robert M. Randolph
Sr. Associate Dean
Office of the Dean of Students
and Undergraduate Education
Massachusetts Institute of Technology

"**T**he graduate school administrator will find that *Helping
Students Adapt to Graduate School:
Making the Grade* frames a com-
mon-sense and rational picture of
graduate students' issues, while providing clear views of the ways to
respond to them. The student affairs
or counseling professional will find
the organization and information of
this publication very useful in
crafting programs of outreach to
and support of graduate students on
campus.

*Helping Students Adapt to Gradu-
ate Schools: Making the Grade* presents cogently a broad overview of
the different aspects of graduate
school and of the diversity that
makes up a graduate student body.
Presented in vignettes, the descrip-
tions of graduate students' challenges have impact, yet they are
realistic, not at all overblown permit-
ting the concerned administrator to
develop an understanding of the
factors presented. The publication
makes a nice case for respecting the
whole person who comes to our
graduate programs as a student and
colleague."

Jane A. Hamblin, JD
*Director of Program Development
Council of Graduate Schools*

The Haworth Press, Inc.

Helping Students Adapt to Graduate School: Making the Grade

Helping Students Adapt to Graduate School: Making the Grade has been co-published simultaneously as *Journal of College Student Psychotherapy*, Volume 14, Number 2 1999.

The *Journal of College Student Psychotherapy* Monographic "Separates"

Below is a list of "separates," which in serials librarianship means a special issue simultaneously published as a special journal issue or double-issue *and* as a "separate" hardbound monograph. (This is a format which we also call a "DocuSerial.")

"Separates" are published because specialized libraries or professionals may wish to purchase a specific thematic issue by itself in a format which can be separately cataloged and shelved, as opposed to purchasing the journal on an on-going basis. Faculty members may also more easily consider a "separate" for classroom adoption.

"Separates" are carefully classified separately with the major book jobbers so that the journal tie-in can be noted on new book order slips to avoid duplicate purchasing.

You may wish to visit Haworth's website at . . .

http://www.haworthpressinc.com

. . . to search our online catalog for complete tables of contents of these separates and related publications.

You may also call 1-800-HAWORTH (outside US/Canada: 607-722-5857), or Fax 1-800-895-0582 (outside US/Canada: 607-771-0012), or e-mail at:

getinfo@haworthpressinc.com

Helping Students Adapt to Graduate School: Making the Grade, by Committee on the College Student, Group for the Advancement of Psychiatry (Vol. 14, No. 2, 1999). "Breaks new ground by giving professors and students a guide to the graduate school experience . . . Thoughtful and clear in both description and prescription; it will benefit both students and their advisors . . . This is a very readable and helpful resource." (Robert M. Randolph, PhD, Senior Associate Dean, Office of the Dean of Students and Undergraduate Education, Massachusetts Institute of Technology, Cambridge, Massachusetts)

Campus Violence: Kinds, Causes, and Cures, edited by Leighton C. Whitaker, PhD, and Jeffrey W. Pollard, PhD (Vol. 8, No. 1/2/3, 1994). *"An indispensable reference work for health educators, administrators, and mental health professionals." (Journal of American College Health)*

College Student Development, edited by Leighton C. Whitaker, PhD, and Richard E. Slimak, PhD (Vol. 6, No. 3/4, 1993). *"Provides college counselors and therapists with some of the most important developmental perspectives needed in todays' work with students." (Educational Book Review)*

College Student Suicide, edited by Leighton C. Whitaker, PhD, and Richard E. Slimak, PhD (Vol. 4, No. 3/4, 1990). *"Belongs in the hands and minds of everyone who works with suicidal students in post-secondary education. . . . Would also be a good text for graduate courses in counseling, social work, psychology, or student services." (Suicide Information & Education Center (SIEC) Current Awareness Bulletin)*

The Bulimic College Student: Evaluation, Treatment, and Prevention, edited by Leighton C. Whitaker, PhD, and William N. Davis, PhD (Vol. 3 No. 2/3/4, 1989). *"An excellent tool for college mental health professionals . . . Practical information and guidelines are provided to help college personnel develop programs for the prevention and treatment of bulimia." (Journal of Nutritional Education)*

Alcoholism/Chemical Dependency and the College Student, edited by Timothy M. Rivinus, MD (Vol. 2, No. 2/3/4, 1988). *"This volume is a compilation of articles on several dimensions of the campus substance abuse problems. . . . A must for the clinician's and the administrator's reading list." (Michael Liepman, MD, Providence VA Medical Center, Rhode Island)*

Parental Concerns in College Student Mental Health, edited by Leighton C. Whitaker, PhD (Vol. 2, No. 1/2, 1988). *"A useful reference for parents and professionals concerning the everyday, yet hardly routine, psychological issues of the college student." (American Journal of Psychotherapy)*

Helping Students Adapt to Graduate School: Making the Grade

Formulated by the Committee on the College Student
Group for the Advancement of Psychiatry (GAP)

Earle Silber, MD, Chairperson

Robert L. Arnstein, MD
Varda Backus, MD
Harrison P. Eddy, MD
Myron B. Liptzin, MD
Malkah Tolpin Notman, MD
Peter Reich, MD
Elizabeth Aub Reid, MD
Lorraine D. Siggins, MD
Morton Silverman, MD
Tom G. Stauffer, MD
Robert E. Wenger, MD

Helping Students Adapt to Graduate School: Making the Grade has been co-published simultaneously as *Journal of College Student Psychotherapy*, Volume 14, Number 2 1999.

The Haworth Press, Inc.
New York • London • Oxford

Helping Students Adapt to Graduate School: Making the Grade
has been co-published simultaneously as *Journal of College
Student Psychotherapy,* Volume 14, Number 2 1999.

Cover design by Thomas J. Mayshock Jr.

Library of Congress Cataloging-in-Publication Data

Group for the Advancement of Psychiatry. Committee on the College Student
    Helping students adapt to graduate school: making the grade/formulated by the Group for
the Advancement of Psychiatry (GAP) Committee on College Students, chairperson, Earle Silber;
committee members Robert L. Arnstein . . . [et al.].
    p. cm.
    "Co-published simultaneously as Journal of college student psychotherapy, volume 14,
number 2 1999."
    Includes bibliographical references (p.) and index.
    ISBN 0-7890-0960-9 (qalk. paper–ISBN 0-7890-0978-1
    1. Universities and colleges–United States–Graduate work–Handbooks, manuals, etc. 2. Graduate
students–Mental health–United States–Handbooks, manuals, etc. I. Title.
LB2371.4.G76 2000

                                                    99-058926

INDEXING & ABSTRACTING

Contributions to this publication are selectively indexed or abstracted in print, electronic, online, or CD-ROM version(s) of the reference tools and information services listed below. This list is current as of the copyright date of this publication. See the end of this section for additional notes.

- *Applied Social Sciences Index & Abstracts (ASSIA) (Online: ASSI via Data-Star) (CDRom: ASSIA Plus)*

- *BUBL Information Service, An Internet-based Information Service for the UK higher education community <URL:http://bubl.ac.uk>*

- *Child Development Abstracts & Bibliography*

- *CNPIEC Reference Guide: Chinese National Directory of Foreign Periodicals*

- *Contents Pages in Education*

- *Educational Administration Abstracts (EAA)*

- *Family Studies Database (online and CD/ROM)*

- *Higher Education Abstracts*

- *International Bulletin of Bibliography on Education*

- *Mental Health Abstracts (online through DIALOG)*

- *Psychological Abstracts (PsycINFO)*

- *Social Services Abstracts*

- *Social Work Abstracts*

- *Sociological Abstracts (SA)*

- *Special Educational Needs Abstracts*

(continued)

Special Bibliographic Notes related to special journal issues (separates) and indexing/abstracting:

- indexing/abstracting services in this list will also cover material in any "separate" that is co-published simultaneously with Haworth's special thematic journal issue or DocuSerial. Indexing/abstracting usually covers material at the article/chapter level.
- monographic co-editions are intended for either non-subscribers or libraries which intend to purchase a second copy for their circulating collections.
- monographic co-editions are reported to all jobbers/wholesalers/approval plans. The source journal is listed as the "series" to assist the prevention of duplicate purchasing in the same manner utilized for books-in-series.
- to facilitate user/access services all indexing/abstracting services are encouraged to utilize the co-indexing entry note indicated at the bottom of the first page of each article/chapter/contribution.
- this is intended to assist a library user of any reference tool (whether print, electronic, online, or CD-ROM) to locate the monographic version if the library has purchased this version but not a subscription to the source journal.
- individual articles/chapters in any Haworth publication are also available through the Haworth Document Delivery Service (HDDS).

Dedication

This report is dedicated to the memory of
Gloria C. Onque, MD,
a cherished friend and colleague,
who made important contributions to this report
through her intelligent and perceptive insights.
We will miss her gracious presence.

Helping Students Adapt to Graduate School: Making the Grade

CONTENTS

ABOUT THE AUTHORS

Robert L. Arnstein, MD, formerly Clinical Professor of Psychiatry at the Yale University School of Medicine, is now an Emeritus Professor. He continues to serve on the Editorial Board of the *Journal of College Student Psychotherapy* of which he was a founding member. He was the Psychiatrist-in-Chief of the Yale University Health Service. The author of numerous papers dealing with critical issues in college student psychiatry, he received awards from the American College Health Association for distinguished service to the field of college mental health.

Varda Backus, MD, a member of Scripps Clinic and Associate Clinical Professor of Psychiatry at the University of California, San Diego, is a member of the American College of Psychiatrists. She was Acting Director of Psychiatry section in the Student Health Center at Stanford and also taught at Harvard University and the State University of New York. She was president of the San Diego Society for Adolescent Psychiatry and has written numerous psychiatric articles.

Harrison P. Eddy, MD, was a psychiatrist in the student health service at Vassar College and treated university students in private practice. He was Clinical Associate Professor of Psychiatry at the New York Medical College and an attending psychiatrist and teacher in the residency program at St. Vincent's Hospital in New York.

Myron B. Liptzin, MD, is Clinical Professor of Psychiatry at the University of North Carolina School of Medicine where he was formerly the Director of Mental Health Services of the Student Health Service. He is a Fellow of the American College Health Association and was also past president of their Section on Mental Health. He has written about student mental health.

Malkah Tolpin Notman, MD, a Training and Supervising Analyst, is president of the Boston Psychoanalytic Institute. Now Clinical Professor of Psychiatry at the Harvard Medical School, she was formerly a faculty member of the Boston University School of Medicine, Professor of Psychiatry at Tufts University School of Medicine and an associate psychiatrist at Wellesley College. She is a past president of the Group for the

Advancement of Psychiatry. She has published articles on reproductive and women's issues, career development and student mental health.

Peter Reich, MD, Chief of the Mental Health Service at the Massachusetts Institute of Technology (MIT) Medical Department, is Professor of Health Sciences and Technology at MIT and Professor of Psychiatry at Harvard University Medical School. He is a member of the Boston Psychoanalytic Institute and Society. He was the Chief of Psychiatry at Brigham and Women's Hospital in Boston. He has served on the editorial board of the New England Journal of Medicine and has published articles dealing with the interface of psychiatry and medicine.

Elizabeth Aub Reid, MD, was a psychiatrist in the Student Health Service at Harvard University where she was the Director of Training and later, Director of Consultation and Liaison to the university. She was a past president of the Boston Psychoanalytic Society and Institute. She has written about student life and consultation on the college campus.

Lorraine D. Siggins, MD, Psychiatrist-in-Chief at the Yale University Health Service, is also Clinical Professor of Psychiatry at the Yale University School of Medicine. She is Supervising Analyst at the Western New England Institute of Psychoanalysis. Her publications include articles about women university students and the role of college mental health consultants.

Earle Silber, MD, a Supervising and Training Analyst in the Washington Psychoanalytic Institute, is a consultant to the Division of Clinical and Behavioral Research of the National Institute of Mental Health and to the National Capital Military Psychiatry Residency Program. He was Clinical Professor of Psychiatry at the Georgetown University School of Medicine and Guest Professor at the Ulm University School of Medicine. He has published articles about adolescent development and the transition from high school to college.

Morton Silverman, MD, is Associate Professor of Psychiatry, Associate Dean of Students in the University and Director of the Student Counseling and Resource Service at the University of Chicago. He is currently the Editor-in-Chief of *Suicide and Life-Threatening Behavior*, the official journal of the American Association of Suicidology. His publications deal with mental disorders in adolescents and young adults and the prevention of alcohol and drug abuse.

Tom G. Stauffer, MD, is Chief Psychiatrist and Director of Health Services at Sarah Lawrence College and Clinical Associate Professor at Cornell Medical College. He is a Fellow of both the American College Health Association and the American Society for Adolescent Psychiatry. He was a consultant to Briarcliff College, supervising psychiatrist at the New York Hospital and past president of the Westchester Psychoanalytic Society.

Robert E. Wenger, MD, conducts a private psychiatric practice which includes the treatment of university students and is currently Director of an inpatient program at the Charter Fairmount Institute in Philadelphia. He was Associate Director of the Student Health Service and Associate Director of the Counseling and Psychological Services at the University of Pennsylvania. He was also Assistant Professor of Psychiatry at the University of Pennsylvania Medical Center.

Preface

Prior to this report by the Committee on the College Student of the Group for the Advancement of Psychiatry (GAP), little has been published about the psychological complexity of the lives of graduate students. The report, which comprises this special issue of the *Journal of College Student Psychotherapy* and is being published simultaneously in book form, describes some of the emotional vulnerability inherent in graduate student study and ways universities can help students function successfully. Graduate students are a vulnerable population, important to the future of our society, and very much at risk at a time when the availability of mental health services on campus is decreasing.

The authors have experience working as psychiatrists in a variety of university mental health settings at Harvard, Yale, Massachusetts Institute of Technology, Sarah Lawrence College, University of Pennsylvania, University of North Carolina, and the University of Chicago. In this capacity they have not only treated graduate students but also served as consultants to faculties and administrators who work closely with graduate students. In addition, they are teachers in medical schools, residency training programs and psychoanalytic institutes, and have considerable experience in the treatment of graduate students in their private practices. Their report is a composite of their experience and describes the complexity of graduate student lives and the necessity of providing students with mental health services and other supports to enable them to cope more successfully with the challenges of graduate school.

The Committee on the College Student has previously published *Sex and the College Student, The Educated Woman, Friends and Lovers in the College Years,* and *Psychotherapy with College Students.* In addition, members of the Committee are contributors to the psychiatric and psychoanalytic literature.

As Editor of the *Haworth College Student Mental Health* book series and

[Haworth co-indexing entry note]: "Preface." Co-published simultaneously in *Journal of College Student Psychotherapy* (The Haworth Press, Inc.) Vol. 14, No. 2, 1999, pp. xvii-xviii; and: *Helping Students Adapt to Graduate School: Making the Grade* (Committee on the College Student, Group for the Advancement of Psychiatry) The Haworth Press, Inc., 2000, pp. xv- xvi. Single or multiple copies of this article are available for a fee from The Haworth Document Delivery Service [1-800-342-9678, 9:00 a.m. - 5:00 p.m. (EST). E-mail address: getinfo@haworthpressinc.com].

the *Journal of College Student Psychotherapy,* I wish to thank all of the members of the GAP Committee, particularly Earle Silber, M.D. who, as Chairperson of the GAP Committee and Guest Editor for this volume, contributed greatly and in myriad ways to its organization and completion, and Robert L. Arnstein, M.D., who is also a founding and continuing Editorial Board member of the *Journal* and helped initiate publication of the GAP report through the *Journal.*

Leighton Whitaker, PhD, ABPP
Editor, JCSP

Group for the Advancement of Psychiatry (GAP)

GAP has a membership of approximately 300 psychiatrists, most of whom are organized in the form of a number of working committees. These committees direct their efforts toward the study of various aspects of psychiatry and the application of this knowledge to the fields of mental health and human relations. Since the formation of GAP in 1946, its members have worked closely with other specialists in related fields of human behavior. GAP is an independent group and its reports represent the composite findings and opinions of its members and consultants.

Helping Students Adapt to Graduate School: Making the Grade was formulated by one of the GAP Committees, the Committee on the College Student. Members of this group have worked as psychiatrists treating graduate students in university student health services as well as in private practice. In addition, committee members have served as consultants to graduate school deans, administrators and faculty. The report is a composite of their experience and describes the complexity of graduate student lives and the necessity of providing students with mental health services and other supports to enable them to cope more successfully with the challenges of graduate school.

The committee members wish to acknowledge their thanks to Howard Blue, MD, for his special contribution to this report and also to Grace Vigilante, MD, Samia Hassan, MD and Doug Monteith, MD, who worked with the committee as Sol W. Ginsburg Fellows. Finally, we wish to express our gratitude and appreciation to Leighton Whitaker, PhD, for his exceptional help in editing the report

[Haworth co-indexing entry note]: "Group for the Advancement of Psychiatry (GAP)." Co-published simultaneously in *Journal of College Student Psychotherapy* (The Haworth Press, Inc.) Vol. 14, No. 2, 1999, pp. xix; and: *Helping Students Adapt to Graduate School: Making the Grade* (Committee on the College Student, Group for the Advancement of Psychiatry) The Haworth Press, Inc., 2000, pp. xvii. Single or multiple copies of this article are available for a fee from The Haworth Document Delivery Service [1-800-342-9678, 9:00 a.m. - 5:00 p.m. (EST). E-mail address: getinfo@haworthpressinc.com].

Introduction

The current mindset of today's graduate and professional student is illustrated by the following bit of grim humor:

> In order to succeed in pursuing higher education,
> the *college student* must figure out how to use the elevator in the campus high-rise building;
> the *master's degree student* must learn to climb up the side of the building;
> but the *Ph.D. student* doing research with a professor must jump over the building in a single bound carrying the professor with him or her.

With a modicum of exaggeration this anecdote captures the overwhelming perceived challenges to achieve that most graduate students experience. This pressure is heightened by the conviction that faculty, fellow students, and families expect even more than students expect of themselves. In reality, graduate students face enormous demands upon their time, energy, intelligence, endurance, patience, and organizational skills. For most students, mastery of these demands leads to a greater sense of competence and self-esteem. However, others respond to these same stresses with considerable distress and emotional problems.

The psychological problems and treatment of *undergraduate* students have been extensively addressed by the GAP Committee on the College Student in its prior publications (GAP Report, 60, 1965; 92, 1975; 115, 1983; and 130, 1990) as well as by many others (for example Farnsworth, 1957; Fry and Rostow, 1942; Blaine and McArthur, 1961; Grayson and Cauley, 1989). Some authors writing about the work of university health centers refer to special problems posed by specific programs for graduate and professional students (Blaine and McArthur, 1961; Bojar, 1961; Babcock, 1961; and Nelson, 1961), but remarkably little has been written about the psychological and

---

[Haworth co-indexing entry note]: "Introduction." Co-published simultaneously in *Journal of College Student Psychotherapy* (The Haworth Press, Inc.) Vol. 14, No. 2, 1999, pp. 1-4; and: *Helping Students Adapt to Graduate School: Making the Grade* (Committee on the College Student, Group for the Advancement of Psychiatry) The Haworth Press, Inc., 2000, pp. 1-4. Single or multiple copies of this article are available for a fee from The Haworth Document Delivery Service [1-800-342-9678, 9:00 a.m. - 5:00 p.m. (EST). E-mail address: getinfo@haworthpressinc.com].

emotional complexity of graduate student lives. Undergraduate distress tends to be more visible, immediate, and noisy.

Although there are no carefully gathered statistics about the number of graduate students who seek therapy, a small survey done by a member of the Committee (Liptzin, 1994) of 20 universities found that, in 60 per cent of the schools, graduate students used campus mental health services more than undergraduates. Faculty and administrators, as well as therapists who work in university settings, should recognize that the problems of graduate students are at least as serious as and often more entrenched than those of undergraduates; consequently, graduate students frequently require more extensive therapy.

At a time when all universities are under severe financial pressures, it may seem paradoxical to write a report that focuses on providing services for a group of individuals which has a history of high achievement. It could be argued that graduate students can probably "manage," so why allocate scarce resources to them? First, high achievement is no guarantee of mental health or stability (Schafer, 1966); second, from a national perspective, this population is important to our country's future. It is essential to realize that, despite their past success, graduate students are as vulnerable as any other group. Graduate students represent our next generation of leaders; a failure to provide adequate resources for their support could result in a tragic loss to the country as a whole if not the world.

Academicians and administrators may regard their mission as solely the education of students. If, however, emotional and psychiatric problems of students are neglected, the result may be higher costs in the long run (Bertocci et al., 1992). When academic performance deteriorates, costly dropouts increase (Pervin et al., 1966). Therefore, it is important to pay attention to the lives of graduate students not only inside the classroom but outside as well.

Universities can enhance the academic performance of graduate students by contributing to the quality of life of students, by supporting their sense of belonging and by providing appropriate support to students' sense of worth. A dean of student affairs can offer direct help to graduate students as well as to various graduate and administrative departments. Such help can begin prior to students arriving through pre-admission mailings and through orientation programs which provide appropriate information about the university. This report describes additional ways that universities can assist in the adjustment of graduate students through direct help to students as well as through indirect help by providing support and resources for individual graduate departments as well as for teachers and advisors in dealing with students.

In addition, psychiatric services which are both available and accessible are a necessary resource for students to cope with the emotional stresses of graduate school. Outpatient care is best provided through a student or university health service located on campus because the providers are more apt to be familiar with the context of the university milieu (Farnsworth, 1957), including an awareness of the particulars of programs of study, their stresses and how they impact on students (Snyder, 1966). Such services not only provide treatment to individuals but also reach out to the university community through the availability of clinicians as consultants to the administration as well. Ideally, these services need to be available not only during academic semesters but also during summer vacations and other breaks in the academic schedule since graduate students continue their research during these times. Off-campus mental health resources are also important to ensure a full range of services for students.

In this report we describe the complex interplay between the university environment and the inner psychological life of its graduate students. We describe the variety of individual characteristics of graduate students and of different programs and describe the complex ways in which students and programs interact to influence the nature of the student's experience. We comment on the potential for infantilization and regression when adults remain in or return to student status. Graduate students are often poor, financially dependent and, in many programs, isolated and uncertain about future career possibilities (Menand, 1996 a & b). Thus, graduate students face psychological as well as intellectual challenges which often require the postponement of mature gratifications. Old conflicts may resurface, potentiating a return to earlier levels of functioning as well as progression toward growth and maturity. Graduate study is an opportunity for both intellectual and emotional growth.

This report is addressed primarily to university faculty and administrators who teach and supervise students in graduate programs. University faculty and administrators are undoubtedly familiar with the challenges and stresses that confront students in graduate programs. The report aims to enlarge their understanding of graduate students by providing a view of students through the eyes of psychiatrists who engage in therapeutic work with them and who act as consultants to universities. We describe experiences with graduate students as whole persons with past histories, differing motivations for attending graduate school and varying levels of emotional maturity. They struggle with conflicts mobilized by being a student while at the same time trying to hold onto and maintain the gains of adulthood (Offer and Sabshin, 1984). We illustrate these problems with case vignettes growing out of our experience. (To insure confidentiality, these examples, while based on real people, are composites and do not describe particular individuals.)

The report may also be of interest to mental health professionals who work with graduate students, by providing them with a view of some of the realities of university life which influence therapeutic work with this population. We aim to promote collaboration among administrators, faculty and mental health professionals in providing support and resources for graduate students to enable them to more successfully help students' adaptations to graduate school.

Finally, it is hoped that this report may be directly useful to graduate students themselves by describing some expectable stresses of graduate study and thereby helping them to put their particular emotional problems in context and to understand that their experiences are neither unique nor immutable.

Chapter 1:

Overview

CHARACTERISTICS OF GRADUATE STUDENTS

Graduate students are not a monolithic group. As individuals, they vary enormously in talents, interests, personality, social skills, financial resources, available support systems and family constellations. Furthermore, the myriad of graduate programs presents distinct challenges and tasks that, in turn, may lead to a variety of emotional stresses and consequent psychiatric crises.

Of course, students in professional schools such as law and medicine will have a markedly different experience than those in other graduate programs such as the liberal arts, sciences or history (Blaine and McArthur, 1961). The program characteristics and academic mission affect the milieu in which the student functions. For example, many law students learn in an academic environment not unlike college with ample administrative support similar to that at a college. In contrast, Ph.D. students in small departments may be immersed in their chosen subject and may have little organized contact with anyone outside their specific field. Part-time students may be enrolled in either a structured professional program or a graduate program that is considerably more flexible in terms of requirements and order of progression. Throughout the report we will use the term graduate student to include both graduate and professional students unless we are commenting on aspects of university life that are specifically related to one or the other.

Graduate students in doctoral programs occupy a critical role as teachers of undergraduates; they often are thrust onto the front lines and forced to deal with the complex emotional problems of undergraduates. If graduate students are having their own emotional difficulties, their problems may have far reaching effects on the undergraduates they teach as well as on faculty who

[Haworth co-indexing entry note]: "Chapter 1: Overview." Co-published simultaneously in *Journal of College Student Psychotherapy* (The Haworth Press, Inc.) Vol. 14, No. 2, 1999, pp. 5-7; and: *Helping Students Adapt to Graduate School: Making the Grade* (Committee on the College Student, Group for the Advancement of Psychiatry) The Haworth Press, Inc., 2000, pp. 5-7. Single or multiple copies of this article are available for a fee from The Haworth Document Delivery Service [1-800-342-9678, 9:00 a.m. - 5:00 p.m. (EST). E-mail address: getinfo@haworthpressinc.com].

5

depend on them as research and teaching assistants. Therefore, it is in the university's self-interest to provide care for this enormously important population on campus.

Graduate students occupy multiple roles, not only within the university but also within society. They must meet the demands of life outside of the classroom, library, or laboratory as husbands, wives, parents, lovers, teachers and perhaps sons and daughters of aging parents.

CHARACTERISTICS OF GRADUATE PROGRAMS

Graduate programs come in many shapes and sizes. Some programs, usually in professional fields, are clearly defined in terms of duration, formal course requirements and regularly scheduled examinations that students must pass to receive a degree. Others have flexible course choice and require a dissertation or a completed project for graduation. What is considered a completed dissertation may depend in large measure on the dissertation advisor who has great power in this context. In contrast, a professional school student is rarely dependent on the approval of a single instructor.

The nature of the curriculum and the support network affect the level of stress that students experience. Professional schools usually have a structured curriculum lasting two to four years, whereas the expected length of time that is needed to complete a graduate school program varies from two years for a master's degree to four to seven or more years for a Ph.D. (Menand, 1996 a & b) The support structure that is available to students within the graduate school proper also varies greatly with the area of study and the size of the department. Furthermore, the value that university officials assign to graduate programs compared to undergraduate studies will affect the atmosphere of the graduate schools and the amount of attention paid to graduate students.

In this regard, professional school training (M.D., M.B.A., J.D.) may be less stressful in some respects and less difficult to decipher then other graduate programs. Professional schools have very clearly demarcated curricula, time frames, sequences, and expectations. At the end of professional school training there may well be a certification examination (licensure for M.D.s, bar exams for J.D.s) that structure the sequence and timing of knowledge acquisition. Coursework is often pre-ordained and only offered in sequence. Here the faculty have clear expectations for performance, faculty/student relationships, and a sense of a superimposed and sequenced beginning, middle, and end to their relationships.

While administrators may view graduate students as independent adults and conclude that they need little from the institution other than academic opportunity, this can also be a rationalization for not providing much in the way of social and academic support. The great diversity among individual students–academic, financial, emotional, and place of origin–is often ignored, leading to the expectation that everyone can fit the same pattern. In departments with small numbers of students or with heavy requirements for individual work, it is common for students to feel isolated and to have less chance of finding compatible friends. This experience contrasts considerably with the collegiality of undergraduate life. Those areas of study that attract international students present even greater problems in socialization because, in addition to difficulties of the program, there are cultural differences to be overcome by both international and U.S. students (GAP Report, 1990; Martinez et al., 1989; Reifler, 1988).

Chapter 2:

Decision to Attend Graduate School

The process by which students make decisions to attend graduate school offers important insights for understanding their subsequent experience. The thinking involved in this decision varies greatly from one student to another. Some students select a career early in life, stay with this choice during college by taking appropriate courses and apply with confidence to the indicated graduate program. For them graduate study is simply an inevitable step on the way to entering their chosen career. Occasionally, such students may postpone attending a graduate program because of financial or family considerations or because of a temporary period of doubt about the wisdom of their decision, but generally graduate school represents a fixed and relatively unconflicted choice.

Many professional careers require a period of special training before practice or advancement. Even in areas such as business, in which many succeed without graduate study, there is an increasing tendency to require a higher level of education for entry level jobs. If a higher degree is not actually required, applicants nonetheless think that such a degree gives them a competitive advantage. The current trend toward greater credentialing may make a degree more important than skills or experience (Menand, 1996a). As more individuals believe this, it becomes a self-fulfilling prophecy; the individual with an excellent record without an advanced degree feels at a disadvantage in competing with someone with the same excellent record and an additional degree. This belief may be undergoing some change in the current decade because there are so many individuals with graduate degrees. Some college graduates may feel that the graduate degree is not worth the two or more years it takes to obtain, and they search for other qualities to make themselves desirable in the job market.

[Haworth co-indexing entry note]: "Chapter 2: Decision to Attend Graduate School." Co-published simultaneously in *Journal of College Student Psychotherapy* (The Haworth Press, Inc.) Vol. 14, No. 2, 1999, pp. 9-11; and: *Helping Students Adapt to Graduate School: Making the Grade* (Committee on the College Student, Group for the Advancement of Psychiatry) The Haworth Press, Inc., 2000, pp. 9-11. Single or multiple copies of this article are available for a fee from The Haworth Document Delivery Service [1-800-342-9678, 9:00 a.m. - 5:00 p.m. (EST). E-mail address: getinfo@haworthpressinc.com].

Several other factors may influence the decision to attend graduate school. Some students select graduate study as a means to delay commitment to a career or more generally to postpone facing entry into "the real world." For some, this delay reflects a realistic, positive assessment of their readiness to commit to a career; for others, it represents a more generalized inability to make commitments that borders on the pathological (Erikson, 1950). For a few individuals, difficulty in commitment is a characterological problem which, in extreme cases, may lead to an extended postponement of any long term decisions about work. Far more often, however, a delay in attending graduate school is an adaptational effort on the part of students to discover or further define their interests, a developmental task that has not necessarily been completed during college. Ideally, these students will clarify their career doubts before beginning graduate study and, if appropriate, return for graduate study with clear goals that will make the academic work meaningful.

Some students may undertake graduate study in lieu of developing a clear future career, or because a faculty advisor encourages them to pursue a particular field. Others turn to graduate school after taking jobs that become unsatisfying or have no potential for advancement. This experience may motivate them to decide that more–or different training–will lead to greater job satisfaction and opportunity. Still others are motivated by a combination of factors and consider graduate study to be generally beneficial even though they are uncertain about a final career goal. It is common for someone to say, "I don't want to practice law, but legal training will be useful whatever I decide to do."

Many college graduates initially do not apply to graduate school but later decide to undertake further study. For some, this may result from a productive use of time in the service of maturation. At the time these students graduated from college they were not ready to make a clear choice of career or to commit to additional years of preparation that were essential (Johnson and Schwartz, 1989). Others need to earn money to pay off college debts or to save money to help support themselves enough to enter a graduate program. It is likely that most postponements are a combination of internal and external factors. Thus, the college senior who has no particular career goal may decide to take a job for a period of time and, while working, may find an interest to pursue that will require further study. Students who have difficulty deciding whether to attend graduate school may find help through an informative publication of The Council of Graduate Schools which provides valuable guidance on career opportunities, how to choose a graduate school, costs, financial aid and other practical information (Hamblin, 1999).

A woman who has married soon after college may find that her life expectations are only partially fulfilled by raising a family, and look forward to the time when her children are in school and she can become involved in a profession. For still others, the so-called "mid-life crisis" (which may occur at any age from 30 to 60) may encourage them to enter a career that differs from their original occupation. Some students find graduate study an enjoyable activity and decide to turn it into a lifelong occupation. Even though most graduate programs have specified time limits, some students are remarkably creative in extending these limits (Menand, 1996b). Certainly the factors influencing a student's decision to attend graduate school are crucial to understanding subsequent emotional problems.

Chapter 3:

The University's Role in Providing Support

OVERVIEW

In many ways, the university is a mini-social organization that can provide a wide range of support for students while they are part of that community. Some educators may feel that the mission of the university is not only primarily academic but also that supportive functions are beyond its scope. This overlooks the fact that when students' psychological well-being is appropriately supported, they experience a level of satisfaction that contributes to their functioning well academically. While the university cannot act as a surrogate family, it can, nevertheless, provide appropriate support to the needs of adult students in promoting a sense of belonging and supporting a sense of worth. In enhancing the quality of life for graduate students, the university also contributes to fulfilling its mission of enhancing academic performance.

Many graduate schools are developing specific programs to support their students' overall psychological well-being (Brennan, 1999). In some universities, each separate school may have a dean for student affairs as well as a dean for academic affairs, and there may be university-wide offices that help students with more general issues such as housing, financial aid and career counseling. Variations in the format of how these functions are designated in a given university depends on the structure and history of the particular university and the specific missions of departments and schools.

Some universities have found that establishing an overarching office of graduate student affairs can be useful in supporting all the individual graduate programs. Acting as a central point and not beholden to any given school or program, it often has a twofold purpose. First, it may be active in initiating

[Haworth co-indexing entry note]: "Chapter 3: The University's Role in Providing Support." Co-published simultaneously in *Journal of College Student Psychotherapy* (The Haworth Press, Inc.) Vol. 14, No. 2, 1999, pp. 13-19; and: *Helping Students Adapt to Graduate School: Making the Grade* (Committee on the College Student, Group for the Advancement of Psychiatry) The Haworth Press, Inc., 2000, pp. 13-19. Single or multiple copies of this article are available for a fee from The Haworth Document Delivery Service [1-800-342-9678, 9:00 a.m. - 5:00 p.m. (EST). E-mail address: getinfo@haworthpressinc.com].

13

projects, such as a student-run café, many social programs, concerts, and athletic events. Ideally it will have some funds to help support student events. Often a very small amount of seed money may allow a project to develop in a manner that would be impossible if there were absolutely no funds. Second, it may provide neutral personnel who can hear and act on reports of disciplinary breaches, on complaints of harassment, and help resolve difficulties within a school or department. It may also take the lead in helping individual deans and/or chairpersons when a traumatic event such as a death occurs on campus. Because the office is not specifically connected with the student's primary locus, it has an enormous advantage in attempting to handle and resolve difficult crises. In some universities such an office includes an ombudsman, who may be a student or a respected faculty member. It is important that students be aware that such offices or resources exist as a place to bring problems and ask for help.

THE TRANSITION INTO GRADUATE SCHOOL: WELCOMING THE STUDENT

The transition into graduate school begins with the application process and the notification that the student has been accepted into a graduate program. How this is done conveys an important message to the student about the university's concern with the student as a person. Hence, it is important to welcome students with an extensive package of informational materials before they arrive on campus. Such "welcoming packets" may include maps of the campus and surrounding neighborhood, information abut local customs, facts about car registration, state driver's license requirements, suggestions about parking, information on banking, lists of cultural and recreational activities and voter registration information.

Students have important concerns about living arrangements and it is helpful for universities to maintain a bureau to inform students about available housing. On-campus housing in the first year may facilitate students' orientation to the university and their particular graduate department. Other specific information is essential for newly arriving students. Does the housing bureau maintain a list of rooms or apartments for rent off-campus? Are there arrangements that provide places to live in exchange for housework? Closely related are questions about eating facilities on or off campus. Students need information about the relative costs of these services since fiscal concerns are crucial for most graduate students. All of this information is essential.

Students are also concerned about the availability of financial support. While some students may have their finances in order before they actually register, many will still need help to make ends meet. It is important to

provide information about university offices which can help w
cial concerns. Students welcome help about part-time work,
be available and how to apply for it. Information about loans and sun..
are also essential for students entering a graduate program.

In addition, such "welcoming packets" might include more specific information about the student's department, the names and numbers of older
students who may serve as guides to orient the student to the department. A
letter from a graduate student already in residence which welcomes the newly
admitted student and outlines specific information can be additionally supportive. The more information provided in advance of the student's arrival on
campus, the more acclimated and less anxious the student will be, particularly
international students who may be entering the United States for the first
time.

In addition to all the problems American students face during the transition into graduate school, international students may have problems adjusting
to new customs, foods and an unfamiliar language that has different rhythms
and vocabulary from their own. Furthermore, they may have no relatives
within visiting distance and be quite lonely and isolated. Universities can
provide lists of faculty and students who speak the language of the international student, can help with information and even the possibility of a home
style meal. Efforts should be made to help with problems about visas and it
may be helpful to have an office on campus that works with the practical
problems of international students. Off-campus international centers should
be listed as a resource as well as local programs teaching English as a second
language. Very often, concerns about health care are a problem and international students should be helped to have appropriate health insurance cover-
age.

Universities need to be certain that all graduate students have health insurance as well as guaranteed *access* to health care (Smith, 1995). For example,
students may be "insured" but may not have access to care while enrolled in
graduate school because their home state health maintenance organization
(HMO) will not cover services in the university community. Obviously, insurance that does not take into account students' changed life situation,
because of external bureaucratic limitations, is no insurance at all. Students
should be alerted to such issues and given advance information about health
care resources in the university and local communities.

Married students may need information about job openings for spouses,
child care facilities and the location and names of both public and private
schools. Students with disabilities need to be aware of what particular supports are available for them.

After students arrive on campus, orientation sessions are essential to trans-
mit the message that the university is committed to ensuring their health and

well-being. Graduate students are reassured when the university informs them not only about academic matters but also about important issues relating to their lives outside the classroom. Some universities provide walking tours of the campus and the area surrounding the university and distribute handbooks with lists of restaurants, bus routes, public transportation facilities and information about campus protective services.

A part of orientation concerns the academic characteristics of the department or program in which the student is enrolled, which may include seminars, symposia and group discussions about career opportunities as well as work and research opportunities within a particular department. Recent graduates may offer important experiences about career paths opened up through particular choices within graduate programs. Orientation includes clarifying the roles of academic advisors and mentors as well as understanding the policies and administrative procedures within departments about grading and academic schedules. Students need to be informed about course selection, rules regarding academic performance, help with access to departmental resources and library facilities. Orientation sessions may be used as opportunities to introduce faculty members and assist in beginning relationships among students, faculty and administrators. Orientation may include some discussion of the academic expectations around plagiarism–inadvertent or advertent–and lab etiquette. It may also be useful to discuss the need for tolerance and general civility, and to review policies in regard to harassment, sexual and general.

PROVIDING ONGOING SUPPORT

Once the initial acclimation and transition process is completed, which may take months, the university can provide continuing support in the nonacademic sphere as well as the academic. Because graduate school can easily lead to isolation, it is important to provide students with opportunity to develop social networks. In addition to sustaining and developing their own individual identity, students also need to feel part of a community. Organized activities can fill a vital role in this process. Religious organizations, clubs such as bridge, chess, and hiking, theater groups, outside speakers and appropriate space for meeting and being with other students can all contribute to the success of social interaction. Some students will seek ways to participate in community service and will meet people with common interests through that channel.

Graduate school can be a very lonely place, and it is not always easy to find a social group that is compatible and accessible. It is helpful for the university to encourage some organized activities, for example, intramural athletic teams open to graduate students or informal social events. Some universities schedule concerts or teas where people can easily drop in and leave. Other universities, recognizing that many graduate students have families with spouses and children, who may have their own feelings of isolation, have conducted a family day with a picnic or an outing with informal games. Some have introduced a centralized snack bar that is open late and forms a central meeting place for students from all parts of the university. Others have offered reduced cost memberships for use of gym facilities.

As the student's academic program develops, official advisors may be assigned and in some cases very close relationships develop. The advisor's role should be clearly defined and not overlap with evaluative or administrative decision-making responsibilities. This can assist the student in making use of the advisor with a greater degree of freedom and trust to discuss academic or personal problems. Support should be provided for advisors and sometimes consultation with mental health professionals can be useful. This may also be provided by scheduling meetings to help with learning *how* to advise, sharing mutual problems that arise in the course of meeting with students and learning when to refer students for professional help. In some universities, mental health professionals are also consultants to the administration. It is vital that such consultation provide help to the administration in ways that do not undermine the students' confidentiality needs or otherwise lessen the availability of mental health resources for students.

Periodic academic progress reviews are essential to help students develop a realistic sense of their own functioning within the graduate school. Clear communication about success as well as problem areas are in the long run supportive to the student. Early identification of difficulties can lead to their being addressed and dealt with at a time when remedial interventions can be available and helpful. In some programs, advanced students may be expected to fill a teaching role, and then the university can provide helpful tutelage in the art of teaching, as well as a resource person with whom they may consult if they run into problems in the teaching experience. Along the way, universities may organize support groups to focus discussion on specific problems, such as those connected with writing a thesis or dissertation.

To attend to the special needs of married graduate students, their spouses and children, universities may provide support groups and assistance with child care, including a day care center. Opening university classes to spouses, either for credit or auditing may increase the spouse's sense of being a part of the university. Many universities have a calendar or bulletin that tells who is visiting on campus and includes other news of the larger university, and spouses should be notified of its existence and how one obtains a copy. Some universities have supported a newsletter aimed specifically at graduate student spouses, which shows them that the university is concerned about their welfare, that they are not alone and that there are other spouses with similar needs. If the university has a website some of this information may be included on the web. Some universities have devised "spouse days" when the spouse can attend class, perhaps meet the professor, and obtain a better sense of how the student member of the couple spends the day.

Access to health care on a confidential basis is a vital service that the university should support either through its own health service or indirectly through contractual arrangement with an outside health group and hospital. Mental health services, provided through health and counseling services, should be available as equally as physical health services. The various modalities should include support groups, individual psychotherapy, medication, couples therapy, academic skills assessment and alcohol and substance abuse counseling. Resources for medical and psychiatric emergency care should also be in place and made clear to students. Treatment provision issues are discussed in more detail later in our report.

University administrators need to be prepared to respond to critical events on campus that involve the student body as a whole, both positive, such as the university receiving an unusual endowment, awards, faculty recognition, or important publications, and disturbing events such as suicide or murder. Consultation with mental health professionals may be useful in organizing meetings, support groups and other resources helpful to graduate students dealing with disturbing events by promoting a sense of community and reducing feelings of alienation and isolation that many graduate students experience.

SUPPORT IN THE TRANSITION FROM GRADUATE SCHOOL

Just as students needed university support to help them with the transition *in* to graduate school, they also require help with the transition *out* of graduate school to the world-at-large. An office of career counseling can give important information about a variety of work situations. For example, post-doctoral fellowships may allow the new graduate to test working in a given area or environment before making a more lasting commitment to a particular career path. Professional schools usually have structured postgraduate opportunities. Students can be helped to become aware of possibilities and deadlines for applications, such as for clerkships for graduating law students or fellowships for other students. Some graduating students will almost immediately be eligible to take licensing examinations and the university or the specific school should inform the student of the particular procedures that must be followed.

In the midst of all these transition pressures, graduates may be trying to decide where they wish to relocate and to determine whether it is possible to find a job in a preferred living area. If students are married, their spouses will presumably have their own opinions about where they would like to live, and weighing the advantages and disadvantages of one location or another may generate considerable stress. Some graduates may have the difficult situation of having few job opportunities in the particular field in which they have their degree. Thus, career counseling will be especially needed.

International students may have the most difficult transitions out of graduate school. If they are going back to their country of origin, the major components of the transition may be decided, but the particular customs of their native country may be more difficult to accept after their experiences in the United States. Students planning to stay in the U.S. may find the transition especially difficult; although the initial adaptation to graduate school may be hard, it is still a relatively tolerant and supportive place, and not exactly representative of the U. S. at large. While the university cannot be expected to solve these problems, it can assist international students to find resources to cope with them. An advisor who has been through the process can also be of special help with the transition.

Chapter 4:

Developmental Issues

A developmental perspective is another key to understanding many of the difficulties that graduate students experience. Most theoretical discussions of the emotional problems of students in higher education focus primarily on traditional undergraduates, ages 18 to 22, late adolescents developmentally making the transition to young adulthood. There is less clarity and consensus about developmental issues in young adults (Settlage et al., 1987). Some mental health professionals argue that graduate students are basically adults; consequently, their emotional problems do not differ from those of individuals of a similar age who are holding down a job or raising a family or both. Our report supports the view that student status during adult years presents unique challenges to continued psychological growth and development. When these special challenges conflict with the developmental tasks involved in reaching adulthood, they may disrupt the attainment of full adult status; or, if those milestones have been attained, the return to student status may trigger a partial regression to earlier developmental patterns. The psychological process of maturation from adolescence to adulthood has been described in different ways (GAP Report, 1990). There is consensus, however, that at a minimum an individual must confront the following issues: (1) separating psychologically from the family of origin, a process that often requires reworking early family conflicts (Blos, 1967); (2) attaining satisfaction in interpersonal relationships including some progression toward a capacity for intimacy (Erikson, 1950); (3) consolidating a satisfying personal and sexual identity; (4) developing a stable character structure which includes sufficient self-esteem, a realistic attitude toward authority, and the ability to commit to a career and usually to a personal relationship (Hartmann, 1958); and (5) developing a satisfying personal code of behavior and a philosophy of life (Witten-

[Haworth co-indexing entry note]: "Chapter 4: Developmental Issues." Co-published simultaneously in *Journal of College Student Psychotherapy* (The Haworth Press, Inc.) Vol. 14, No. 2, 1999, pp. 21-34; and: *Helping Students Adapt to Graduate School: Making the Grade* (Committee on the College Student, Group for the Advancement of Psychiatry) The Haworth Press, Inc., 2000, pp. 21-34. Single or multiple copies of this article are available for a fee from The Haworth Document Delivery Service [1-800-342-9678, 9:00 a.m. - 5:00 p.m. (EST). E-mail address: getinfo@haworthpressinc.com].

berg, 1968). All these aspects of maturation will be experienced in relation to an internally-held vision of the life-cycle that is shaped by the culturally determined expectations, as well as the timing of life events. Neugarten (1979) has advanced the concept that every culture and many subcultures have a more or less fixed view of the order and age at which certain life events are expected to occur.

Some of these "normative" ages are based on biological factors such as the childbearing limits on women, but most are the result of preference and tradition. Today there is greater leeway for variations to occur, and some of the standards are changing, but there are still approximate "time standards" that individuals measure themselves against. They tend to mark their developmental progress by what seems age-appropriate and to judge the experience according to traditional age expectations. The timetable is subtly transmitted by the culture in which an individual lives, and the individual may be only dimly aware of its existence and importance in psychological terms. For example, in the Victorian middle class, men were expected to postpone marriage until they were financially able to support a family, whereas women were expected to marry early and unmarried women were considered "old maids" by their early 20s. Such age expectations of marriage change when both partners expect to work and pursue careers. Today, financial security may prove less important in determining marriage than in the past, but may still be an important factor in determining the ability to pursue graduate study.

Education today is no longer as rigidly confined to specific age groups as it once was (Slotnick et al., 1993). Nevertheless, many students still choose to postpone marriage, children and a relatively permanent home base in favor of education. Sometimes students' lives necessitate a psychological change such as needing to delay independence that, in turn, causes a shift in immediate goals that "upsets" the timetable. The more significant question is whether these postponements are temporary or reflect internal inhibitions about progression toward adulthood. The answer probably depends on where the individuals–who happen to be graduate students–are in terms of their psychological development and life stage. Returning to or continuing in the status of a student may conflict with the achievement of expectable developmental tasks such as autonomy in relation to parents and the and commitment to an intimate relationship with a partner. Such conflicts may contribute to emotional problems of decreased self-esteem, depression and anxiety. These problems may be exacerbated by such external factors as lack of money and the unavailability of career opportunities. These external concerns have greatly increased in the 1980s and 1990s. Ready employment for those with advanced degrees no longer exists. Teaching jobs are in very short supply; even industry has an excess of Ph.D.s (Menand, 1996a) and research funds have been severely curtailed.

SEPARATION AND REWORKING OF OLD FAMILY ISSUES

While graduate students do have a measure of autonomy in many of their programs, in general a rather strict hierarchical system prevails which inevitably affects students' feelings about their status, values, maturity, and even identity. Whether a graduate student is 22 years old and a recent college graduate, or 42 and returning to academia following many life experiences, the return to student status often causes, and indeed sometimes compels, the reactivation of earlier family issues (Blos, 1967). While this may be painful, at the same time it can be growth promoting for a student to struggle with such conflicts again and to find more adaptive ways of dealing with them than may have been possible at an earlier time of life.

For example, the way in which a student fits into the configuration of the family of origin, how much self-worth the student had developed, how achievement was viewed by important family members, or how sibling competition was expressed are all early experiences that have the potential for reenactment and reworking in the graduate environment.

In significant respects the faculty fill the roles of parental authority and other students may be equated to siblings. Early conflicts may be repeated in a student's need for approval and appreciation, or in their choice of a mentor (Moran, 1992). The manner in which a student seeks knowledge and instruction, recognition and appreciation, and, perhaps more desperately, a faculty member to act as a guide are all influenced by early developmental history. There are students with brimming confidence and students overcome with shyness; each of them approaches the scholarly task in his or her own unique way. Sometimes, a particular faculty advisor will be experienced as an authoritarian parent by one student while another may see the same person as a loving, overly permissive parent who does not insist on excellence.

Sibling rivalry issues can emerge in the intense competition for grades and recommendations, the ultimate symbols of success in graduate school. To students' surprise, ways of handling old childhood rivalries may occur as students find themselves acting and reacting toward their classmates as they did to siblings long ago. While collegiality is proclaimed as a desirable aspect of graduate study, issues of dominance and submission are omnipresent whether in the intellectual, social or political sphere.

Similarly, earlier struggles about autonomy may be replayed, even ones that go back to early childhood and which have already been revisited once in adolescence (Blos, 1967). They may resurface now because students who are chronologically, and largely psychologically, independent adults, are in an environment that often does not acknowledge their independence and may even foster dependency and a reversion to a "childlike" state. Understanding and working with the dynamics of these complex dependency relationships can be very difficult, especially because they often shift over time. Having mastered the age-appropriate developmental tasks of separation and individ-uation, healthy graduate students may well find themselves frustrated and bewildered by the realization that this process must begin anew in yet another setting with yet another set of authority figures. These students have to learn to pace themselves and be patient with the process, because they cannot move too quickly toward equality if the program demands a certain sequence of courses, seminars, experiences, and milestones.

The demands of graduate school can hamper students' sense of autonomy and independence, whether they have had an uninterrupted education, or have returned to school after having worked for a few years and supported themselves or their family. Actually, students may be caught between being subject to fostered dependency on the one hand and being left entirely on their own on the other. The following vignette illustrates some of the devel-opmental struggles that ensued when it was necessary for a student to depend on her parents financially in order to continue her education:

Cathy, a 28-year-old medical student with a history of anorexia nervosa sought treatment for disabling feelings of depression. She had put her-self through college in six years, worked for a couple of years thereafter and then applied to medical school. She had hoped to get scholarship aid in medical school, but was turned down. Her father, a physician, offered to help financially, and she reluctantly accepted.

Cathy was leery about becoming financially dependent on her par-ents for whom the tuition was a financial burden despite their income level. She felt emotionally tied to them and found it hard to "sever the umbilical cord." She felt beholden to them for their financial support and phoned them several times per week to discuss diagnostic questions with her physician father. After hanging up, she felt frustrated, torn, and patronized but, despite repetitions of this sequence, she continued to call frequently and invite her parents' overinvolvement. She felt "in-debted and guilty" if she expressed dissatisfaction with her parents and found it difficult to acknowledge angry feelings within herself. She wondered if severing the financial bond by taking out loans would provide some relief.

Cathy was clearly struggling to achieve a sense of autonomy and independence. Her battle with anorexia nervosa during her teens repre-sented a struggle to assert control of her own body and highlighted the depth of family enmeshment and her difficulties in separation. During her college and working years these conflicts were dormant, but they reemerge forcefully under the stress of medical school and financial dependence, a combination of internal conflicts and external problems. One wonders how much of the difficulty was Cathy's and how much her father's reluctance, for his own unconscious reasons, to see her become more independent.

Cathy's therapist helped her to appreciate that her relationship with her father had both positive and negative aspects; it provided her with great strength, but kept her in a subordinate position which she both wanted and resented. Cathy's understanding and greater acceptance of her own internal struggle reduced the intensity of her anger with her father. Her insight strengthened her growing *inner* sense of independence.

The manner in which students deal with various ongoing (and, in some sense, lifelong) developmental themes in the graduate school environment may heavily influence the strengthening of self-esteem and how subsequent life challenges are met. Some individuals become more assertive, some more cautious; more passive, acquiescent, and compliant; and some become easily depressed. Some insulate themselves from organizational "systems" which are in a way reminiscent of "family"; while others learn to manipulate the system with or without repeating old patterns. Students may grow proficient at negotiating aspects of power, achievement, narcissism and interpersonal transactions, and are tempted to use these techniques when they see that self-aggrandizing strategies can be successful in helping career advancement.

INTERPERSONAL RELATIONSHIPS

During the late adolescent and early adult years students have ample opportunity to meet a variety of people and to develop personal relationships, including relatively close ones. In school it is generally safe to experiment with new kinds of relationships and, in the process, to develop and mature. To the extent that friendships and romantic involvements prove rewarding and enduring, students grow in self-confidence, and, usually, progress down the path toward intimacy (GAP Report, 1983). In experiencing these relationships, students test their competency and capacity for gratification as well as the degree of trust and safety achieved in the presence of another. "Love" becomes better defined and its limits perceived in more realistic terms. "Commitment" becomes a concept that one can comprehend, consider, and perhaps even contemplate.

Being in graduate school, however, may have a paradoxical effect on many of these ongoing interpersonal experiments. On the one hand it may encourage them by providing easy arrangements for living together and provide examples of those who have achieved some success in relationships; on the other hand the need for geographic relocation may be the most tangible example of an external obstacle to a sustained relationship. The struggles to maintain career aspirations and the competitive atmosphere that often prevails in graduate environments may run counter to the preservation of affectionate or supportive ties. The following vignette illustrates a frequent problem that occurs when two students in the same field develop a close relationship:

> Jane was a fourth-year graduate student in psychology attempting to complete the first two chapters of her dissertation. She came to the Mental Health Service with complaints about her inability to work efficiently and with symptoms of depression and anxiety. On further evaluation she revealed that she had been living with a fellow graduate student who was also studying psychology. Part of her current distress apparently related to her uncertainty about the future of this relationship.
>
> Both Jane and her boyfriend were looking for teaching positions, but since the opportunities were limited, Jane was concerned that they would not be able to find jobs in the same location. She feared that, as a result, the relationship would inevitably break up. Jane was not even sure that her boyfriend wished to continue the relationship; in her more depressed moments she wondered if he might be relying on the job dilemma as an excuse for leaving her. She questioned the desirability of finishing her dissertation and wondered if she would not be better off giving up on the prospect of a career as a psychologist.
>
> Jane came from a comfortable family and had always been a good student. She grew up in competition with an older sister who was valedictorian of her class and was proceeding steadily toward a highly-paid career as a lawyer. Jane's parents made every effort to be equally admiring of Jane and her sister. Jane, however, felt strongly that the occasional remarks about the differential earning potential of lawyers and professors represented their greater approval of her sister. In therapy Jane described feeling competitive with her boyfriend and was not quite sure whether the competitive strivings were hindering her ability to progress in her work.
>
> It was apparent that Jane was experiencing deeply entrenched internal problems that were stirred up by the realistic external ones. Jane became aware of serious inhibitions that she felt would preclude her making a commitment to any relationship. Some of what she attributed to her boyfriend's difficulties also represented aspects of her own problems. She found it helpful to face her own long-standing difficulties about commitment that she had avoided recognizing before entering therapy. With this clarification, Jane accepted the recommendation of her therapist for a referral for more intensive long term treatment. In a subsequent follow-up note to her therapist, Jane said that while she had

been able to complete her thesis, she and her boyfriend were not in the same city and were still struggling with the future of their relationship.

This example illustrates the complex interplay of external factors in this graduate student's life with her internal struggles resulting from her psychological development. While a couple in graduate school may share mutual intellectual interests, competition and comparison may interfere with deeper commitment to the relationship and with the attainment of academic goals. These same factors may mask internal inhibitions about commitment as well. For example, a male graduate student may have difficulty sustaining a relationship with a woman who is clearly more capable than he; unconsciously he may want to put obstacles in her way.

Furthermore, it is realistically more difficult for two people in the same field to find comparable and appropriate academic jobs in the same geographic location than it is for people in two unrelated fields. Until relatively recently, some universities had nepotism rules that precluded hiring couples (Gibbons, 1992) and the increase in the number of two-career couples, especially in the same overloaded field, has made this an especially difficult situation.

The very nature of graduate study requires privacy and relative isolation which may lead to neglect and stunting of friendships, to undermining of romantic liaisons, and to a deep sense of loneliness with all its attendant sequela including depression. One often sees this clinical phenomenon in the graduate population. Depression and social isolation are the most common complaints of graduate students seeking help with emotional problems. They are especially prevalent among those candidates for a Ph.D. whose dissertation research is often a solitary endeavor (Nelson, 1961). They have little time for socializing if long hours must be spent in the library or laboratory, or in writing. For obvious reasons, isolation is less a problem in professional school, where much of the work is done in groups.

IDENTITY FORMATION

The psychological task of identity consolidation is most often associated with the late adolescent years (Erikson, 1968). It is not simple because individuals inevitably display a series of partial identities, and the process of consolidation implies that individuals have achieved a certain prior stability of self (including gender and sexual orientation), a sense of connection to their *past*, a reasonably familiar internal *present* and moderately well defined aspirations toward the *future*.

Further aspirations evolve throughout one's life, but the initial phase of identity consolidation is often well developed by the time students graduate from college. Some graduate school applicants do not have this sense of consolidation and thus may choose continuing in school, consciously postponing a career decision in order to leave open possibilities. Or, the process of delay may be more malignant and result in what Erikson (1968) has called "identity diffusion."

The following vignette illustrates the interaction between an individual's attempt to consolidate his identity and unresolved family problems that were in all probability unconsciously interfering with the consolidation process:

> Bill, a 24-year-old, second year medical student, sought psychotherapy to "deal with the fact that both of my parents are alcoholic." He found himself feeling "down" after he transferred to a medical school far from home in order to live with his girlfriend. Bill listed a series of concerns: lack of confidence; guilt about not being sure that he wanted to marry his girlfriend; not feeling "proud" of himself; not wanting to socialize; worry that he would become like his father who "blurts out hurtful things"; and, most important, conflict about whether to try to get his mother into an alcohol treatment program. Bill explained that he had been successful and content in the past because he had "tunnel vision," and just "didn't deal with anything," but that, he began to feel troubled and at a loss since he could no longer deny the severity of his mother's alcoholism. His anxiety did not affect his grades and he continued to receive honors on his exams.
>
> In psychotherapy, Bill described his mother in glowing terms. She is "the best person in the world." She "would give you the shirt off of her back," and is self-sacrificing to the point that she has "no self." Bill, the oldest of four sons, had been the closest to her, "her main support." Upon transferring to another medical school, he informed her that he would no longer speak to her on the phone if she were drunk. As a result they had had almost no contact which Bill experienced as a painful loss. Bill revealed that his mother's alcoholism had progressed to the point that she had threatened to harm his 13 year-old brother. He wondered whether to do a family intervention. When he went home for Christmas he finally decided to do so and felt considerable relief.
>
> As therapy progressed, Bill wondered why he discussed his father so rarely and did not try to get him into treatment for his alcoholism. He recalled an incident when he was 13 years old and his parents were separated. One day the father appeared and hauled the drunken mother to the bedroom. Bill found it "disgusting"–he could "feel what he was doing to her." He described the father as "mean, a professional mess" and a man who "hates doctors."
>
> Bill was not ready to address his complex feelings about his parents before he began to establish a professionally and personally indepen-

dent life. Without realizing it, he had delayed dealing with problems of separation and autonomy until he was accepted at medical school and had assured himself that he could cope with the work. Once he had accomplished these two goals, other developmental processes unfolded. Because of the limited focus of Bill's brief therapy, the relationship between Bill's choice of medicine as a career and his comments about his father who "hates doctors" was not explored. One can speculate that such a connection existed since choice of career is multi-determined; Bill's dislike for, and, in a sense, defiance of his father may have been one of the factors in his choice. Brief therapy assisted Bill in achieving a greater degree of psychological separation from his parents, to "let go" of them internally and consolidate his own life, which, in turn, facilitated greater commitment to his relationship with his girlfriend.

STABILIZATION OF CHARACTER STRUCTURE

The term "character" is a somewhat elusive term that is used to describe a variety of psychological aspects of an individual's psychodynamic functioning. It refers primarily to relatively stable aspects of the personality that gradually over time form rather fixed patterns and establish a psychic structure. This structure includes characteristic responses to stress, dominant moods, attitudes toward work, ways of relating to people, and such intangibles as a sense of humor and how one handles anger. The concept of psychic structure overlaps with the notion of identity and includes both positive and negative aspects of an individual's functioning. Typically, character structure is quite difficult to change.

Some graduate students become better educated than their parents and have potential for greater success than their parents. If they are uncomfortable about surpassing their parents, they may have difficulty consolidating their work identity as the following vignette illustrates:

> Kenneth was a fourth-year graduate student in English. He came to the university medical service because of very upsetting headaches. Although his symptoms mimicked those of migraine, they did not respond to routine migraine treatment and thus which called into question the diagnosis. He was then referred for psychiatric evaluation by an internist who said that Kenneth looked very calm even though he described the symptoms as "very distressing."
>
> Kenneth came from a small midwestern town and had been an excellent high school student and outstanding hockey player. A friend suggested that he apply to a highly selective college, and he was accepted

on a scholarship. His family was pleased though his schooling produced a financial strain even with the aid of the scholarship. But when he decided to work part-time and not go out for hockey, his father, a middle manager in a manufacturing company and an avid sports fan, was disappointed and said so. As a freshman Kenneth had developed acute obsessive-compulsive symptoms (which were quite unlike the symptoms he developed in graduate school), entered psychotherapy briefly, his symptoms remitted, and he did well academically and socially. Uncertain as to what he wanted to do after college, he accepted, almost by default, a scholarship offer for graduate school in English. His family took a dim view of his choice which they saw as totally impractical.

Kenneth re-entered therapy in graduate school and continued until his graduation. His symptoms fluctuated considerably. He had one or two severe episodes of headache which seemed to coincide with his achievement of significant academic milestones. Any suggestion of success sent his anxiety soaring. Therapy revealed that this sequence was related to his fears of distancing himself from his family, as well as feeling that he did not deserve success and recognition. It was apparent that this repetitive pattern of headaches was related to early difficulties with separation and the guilt related to competitive strivings, particularly with his father. He expressed feelings of guilt that he had become financially independent of his family, and that even in his student status was able to enjoy luxuries they could not.

In therapy, which lasted more than two years, Kenneth was able to understand how he experienced external events and to recognize how his inner conflict was connected with his symptomatic episodes. This gave him some sense of control over his emotions and, although his symptoms persisted, they were less frequent and severe. By the time he had completed his degree he had established a reasonably clear, less conflicted and more stable sense of himself.

There are various ways to work out old family issues. Many are temporary or trial solutions which can be given up when they are no longer useful after graduate school is completed. For some students, however, the old modes of adaptation persist and thus become important elements in the adult personality. In Kenneth's case, while he continued to experience conflicts about achievement, they were less intense as a result of his therapy. He became more comfortable about his choice of vocation and consolidated his work identity with less interference from old patterns.

The following vignette illustrates a repetitive maladaptive reaction to authority figures:

Donna was a 23-year-old senior law student who sought therapy in November because she could feel her body "sinking into sadness." She was tired all the time, had difficulty getting out of bed in the morning, gained some weight, had crying spells, felt unattractive, did not want to go out, study, or apply for jobs. Her boyfriend had recently broken up with her, and without a companion, she felt "insecure, empty, and unsafe." She found these feelings distressing because she aspired to be a self-sufficient woman whose self-esteem is derived from work and not based on a relationship with a man. Donna wanted to maintain a state of being an "up, charming, fun, successful, spontaneous, gregarious person." In describing her painful feelings, she said, "It's so silly, I have everything. There's no reason to be upset." She felt dissatisfied with her work even though she was in the top third of her law school class.

Donna laughed as she recalled her childhood: "screaming, throwing things, and physical fights among very loving and close, but just emotional" family members. Her mother was diagnosed as having a recurrent major depressive disorder and a psychiatrist had prescribed antidepressant medications for an older sister. Donna's parents divorced when she was 19. She described her mother when not depressed as "vivacious, fun, my best friend." She described her father as "uptight about money" although the family was wealthy. As a child, Donna was nervous about asking for money. She would itemize her monetary needs and try to make do with the bare minimum.

Her disabling symptoms fit the criteria for a diagnosis of a major depression. She was started on antidepressant medication, and responded relatively quickly; though this relieved her depressive symptoms, she continued to experience other difficulties. During psychotherapy sessions, Donna discussed her fears concerning future jobs and present school responsibilities. Preparing assignments for a judge involved "agonizing procrastination," "panic attacks," and worries that "it won't be good enough," to the point of not being able to get the work done on time. She had neglected to prepare for her first job interview at a competitive law firm and felt that she came across as "flaky." She felt so distraught afterwards that she cried all the way home. She had put the interview out of her mind until the last minute because thinking about it made her too nervous.

When offered a job soon afterward by another firm, Donna had misgivings about how she handled the salary negotiation. She was asked how much she wanted, and she handed over an itemized list of her minimum expenses, thinking that this was a good way to have a friendly, honest relationship. They gave her the amount described, but she became quite distressed because she realized that she had neglected to include the taxes she would have to pay and her health insurance. She did not see how she could manage with the amount agreed upon, but she felt she could not reopen the issue.

Through therapy Donna came to understand that her current unhappiness had two roots: one was the old pattern of denial and self-defeating behavior, understandable in terms of her difficult home situation during her childhood, but not really relevant to the present; the other, given her family history, a biologic predisposition to depression. By understanding the complex relationship between her past and present difficulties, she was able to control her reactions and to remove many of her self-imposed obstacles to success. She became educated about her depression and accepted the need for periodic psychiatric care and continuing on medication.

The vignette illustrates two important aspects of Donna's character structure: her attitude toward authority, learned through her interactions with her father which adversely influenced her salary negotiation, and her perfectionism, which hampered her in completing work. She must have also unconsciously internalized an attitude at home that her self-esteem should depend on her relationships with men even though consciously she wanted to base her self worth on her professional accomplishments at work. Donna minimized the severity of her depressive episodes, probably because of her fear of becoming like her mother, and delayed seeking psychiatric care. The developmental problems illustrated in this case are not unique to adults in graduate school and may occur in other settings. The stresses of law may be similar generally to those encountered in the business world.

Antidepressant medication was a necessary and significant part of this student's treatment. It is important to note, however, that not all patients will experience such a rapid salutary response with minimal side effects. Although the newer drugs, in particular the selective serotonin re-uptake inhibitors (SSRIs), are well tolerated, some students do not do well on SSRIs and medication must be changed to another drug. Others find that the new drugs are too expensive and prefer a drug available in generic form.

When medication is indicated, selecting the proper dose of the right medication may require combining therapeutic efficacy with minimal side effects. This often takes time. While some studies have shown that there may be no statistical significance in outcomes over time for depressed patients treated with psychotherapy alone, drugs alone or with both in combination, other studies and our own experience present considerable evidence that combining medication with psychotherapy is the most desirable therapeutic approach, especially for students with more severe or recurrent major episodes of depression (Miller et al., 1996, Hirschfeld and Schatzberg, 1994, Thase et al., 1997, Paykel, 1995, Karasu, 1990). Psychotherapy alone may be sufficient in treating milder forms of depression. Sometimes, in working with depressed students who are stuck in situations such as a prolonged lack of productivity or not sleeping after the break up of a significant relationship, using medication for a brief period can be very helpful.

The treatment of students who have a history of alternating symptoms of depression and manic behavior is much more complex. It usually involves establishing a supportive therapeutic relationship and the combined use of antidepressants with other medications to stabilize mood swings. The student's clinical course must be carefully monitored, medications carefully selected and the doses adjusted accordingly. Lastly, any depressed student with severe depressive or psychotic symptoms may be in danger of suicide and must be followed very closely and/or hospitalized expeditiously to provide for protection and needed structure (Whitaker, 1990).

A PHILOSOPHY OF LIFE

One task in reaching adult status is becoming able to conceive satisfactory life goals–goals that in some sense act as a guide or steering mechanism through life. They can be thought of as a philosophy of life or a personal set of values. The specific application of these values, of course, may change, but the mind-set remains and provides a vision of the future that helps to determine choices and decisions. This task has been described by Hartmann (1958) and Wittenberg (1968), and is exemplified by the following case:

> Marie is a 24-year-old law student who, after graduating summa cum laude from a prestigious college, taught in a small private school for a year while living with her then boyfriend. When he decided to move, she traveled with him to a Caribbean island where they both taught school for a year, but the relationship ended, and she returned to her parents' home. She then worked as a paralegal while applying to programs in both law and education. She began dating a young man whom she had initially dated in high school. At that time she had broken up the relationship because she disapproved of his use of illegal drugs. He continued to use drugs and she maintained her disapproval. Nevertheless, they were back together, and she was alternately ecstatic and distraught about the relationship.
>
> Marie had entered therapy briefly in her senior year of high school; although her ostensible complaint then was a relationship crisis, it was evident that she also needed some help in choosing a college and leaving home. She was then a very bright, but extremely anxious young

woman. Six years later her return to therapy was again motivated by confusion in a relationship, but this confusion was clearly a more significant problem having to do with her basic values. She was better able to see the confusion as existing within herself–not just emanating from persons outside. Treatment sessions were spent exploring her difficulties, clarifying her values, and considering her choices based on these values in her life ahead.

This vignette illustrates the fact that, if certain problems are not worked through and at least partially resolved, the same problems may recur later. In both instances, Marie's anxieties were precipitated by relationship difficulties, but in each instance these difficulties appeared to mask more fundamental conflicts. In the first instance, Marie received help in making a decision to leave for college, but a similar relationship problem arose in law school and was more difficult to resolve without longer term therapy. Marie's treatment eventually enabled her to feel more confident about seeking a relationship with a man whose values were more compatible with her own.

Chapter 5:

General Aspects of Graduate School Life

Certain general aspects of life in institutions of higher learning take on special prominence in graduate school. They will be discussed in some detail because one or another aspect is frequently a factor in an individual student's development of emotional difficulties. These aspects include gender issues, faculty-student relationships, financial issues and postponement issues, all of which have probably always been present, but certain changes in the graduate school population, such as the increased number of women and older students, have made them more critical.

GENDER ISSUES

There are some ways in which men and women face different issues in graduate school (Notman, 1991; Ritvo, 1976; Gilligan, 1982; Miller, 1976; Gold, 1978). One obvious major difference is the biological age limit for women in regard to childbearing. Often women graduate students choose to postpone marriage and children in deference to career pressure and, if they do, they are faced with anxiety about the difficulty and possible hazard of conceiving at an older age. If they do not, children become part of the complex of juggling work and home responsibilities. Although it is certainly possible and more common than it was a generation ago for fathers to share some part of these responsibilities, it still is the woman who becomes pregnant, bears the child, and, in most families, is the primary caretaker especially in the child's early years (Amato, 1992). Many women define themselves in terms of their family role. Although this may be less true in graduate student families than for women in more traditional families, it is still usually the

[Haworth co-indexing entry note]: "Chapter 5: General Aspects of Graduate School Life." Co-published simultaneously in *Journal of College Student Psychotherapy* (The Haworth Press, Inc.) Vol. 14, No. 2, 1999, pp. 35-56; and: *Helping Students Adapt to Graduate School: Making the Grade* (Committee on the College Student, Group for the Advancement of Psychiatry) The Haworth Press, Inc., 2000, pp. 35-56. Single or multiple copies of this article are available for a fee from The Haworth Document Delivery Service [1-800-342-9678, 9:00 a.m. - 5:00 p.m. (EST). E-mail address: getinfo@haworthpressinc.com].

35

woman who must resolve the societal contradictions involved in balancing work and family. The woman is expected to arrange for child care and for job adaptations such as time off while her children are young.

These contradictions frequently evoke difficult conflicts and feelings that are experienced as unacceptable. Women may feel they want to be at home, and, therefore, they are seen as not "serious" enough about their work or career. If they want to work, it can appear that they are neglecting their family. When the family faces choices, such as whose career needs are primary and who makes the sacrifices, social expectations still are that the woman makes the sacrifices. Although contemporary graduate students in many instances do attempt to work things out in a more egalitarian way, the woman's relationship to her family is usually one in which she takes more immediate responsibility for day-to-day management and decisions.

When a woman decides to postpone having a child until completing graduate study that takes her into her late thirties, fertility problems may arise. Although the evidence is not clear, there are some indications that postponing childbearing is associated with increased infertility. Many women in their twenties and thirties feel that they do not want children, but later change their minds. Women also frequently worry about the risks of childbearing at an advanced age and this concern influences how many children they want or will have. Inevitably, these issues interact with their career ambitions.

Such concerns also affect men. It is traditional for a man to view his working outside the home as consistent with his role as a father providing financial support for his family. As these traditional role definitions change, however, men as well as women may expect themselves to participate more actively as primary care givers. Thus, male graduate students may experience similar conflicts about juggling academic work with child care but usually not as intensely as women do.

Every couple is challenged to work out how this role juggling can play out in daily living, but good models are lacking. For the woman, it means giving up some of her internal expectations to be the fully responsible one. For the man it means holding on to his internal sense of masculinity while taking on responsibilities and roles traditionally considered feminine. Graduate students may be ahead of the mainstream culture in these respects, so that one sees more innovative adjustments, both in behavioral and in psychological terms, than one might in the population at large.

Competition in graduate programs often forces students to confront the stereotypes of what is considered masculine and what is considered feminine in a given field of study. Though these ideas vary with subcultures and from era to era, if a female student feels that her goals and behavior are "unfeminine" by the standards she grew up with, she may feel self-doubt and conflict. The value that male intellectual ability receives, and the often concomitant depreciation of female intellectual ability are frequently replayed in classrooms in a fashion not unlike that which occurred at home. Friendships and romantic relationships can complicate these conflicts. Speaking up in class, asking questions after class, and requesting special arrangements may all be actions that individuals feel must be congruent with their views of what is acceptable behavior for themselves as men or women.

It is clear that there are differences in how certain behaviors are judged depending whether the behavior is initiated by a man or a woman. This fact has considerable impact on the climate for women engaged in graduate study, and indirectly on their internal development. In all but a few instances women are entering what has until recently been a man's world with rules developed by men about how the game is played. For women, then, it may be necessary to adapt to this world and compete in ways that do not conform to their upbringing or that may be in direct conflict with earlier internalized values. For example, many young women have been taught explicitly or by example that it is important to be "good girls" and to perform well. These may have become their dominant conscious goals. In graduate school such women experience considerable conflict when forced to compete actively for grants, teaching jobs or fellowships since simply performing well and being part of a "team" no longer assures success (Nelson, 1961). She can inhibit her competence or feel anxious about it, but neither solution is really acceptable. To cope with this dilemma, women's colleges have often been helpful to young women by providing support and models for women who desire to be achievers. For graduate study the choice of a single sex school virtually does not exist.

Gender issues may also influence students' choice of priorities. Although men may desire and hope for relationships that include affection and intimacy, having relationships and to some extent defining themselves by relationships seems to be more important for women than men (Gilligan, 1982). The male stereotype suggests that men focus more on success in their chosen career so as to achieve recognition and possibly public acclaim. It may even include a belated sense of inner triumph related to achievement in a sibling rivalry left over from childhood.

The competitive elements in graduate school are usually more compatible with stereotypical male socialization which rewards emphasis on winning and is tolerant of overt aggression to that end. Typically, male graduate students are likely to feel anxiety related to competition with other males which resonates with battles with siblings or rivalry with fathers. Since women as a rule put more emphasis on nurturing social interaction than men, female graduate students are more likely than men to experience anxiety about expressing aggression for fear of destroying or losing a romantic relationship. As a result, women students can find themselves in competitive relationships for which their mothers and grandmothers did not provide models.

In many graduate programs women students report problems in finding mentors (Gibbons, 1992). It is often possible to find a supportive professor, or thesis advisor who actively promotes women as long as they are still students, but once they have completed their degree, the relationship may change, and, when it comes to the next level, namely recommendations for jobs, and inclusion in the networks which are important to career development (such as invitations to conferences or a chance to present papers) many women report feeling out of the loop. These feelings may be reinforced by women graduates who come back to the school and report the difficulties that they are encountering in the field (Healy, 1992). Furthermore, the relative absence of women who occupy visible leadership positions in academia or beyond conveys a message that it is difficult to combine a leadership position with a family (GAP Report, 1975).

Many young women students feel that the battles for equality have been won and, with regard to admission to graduate programs, this seems to be true; it may be less true, however, as one progresses along an academic career path (Barinaga, 1992). In the academic world there are indications that women are hired and advance early but are less likely to be given tenure. Evidence of limits and the "glass ceiling" can come at various points during graduate school if women are not considered for specific opportunities.

It is extremely helpful to have several women with differing life patterns as potential role models available in each program to indicate that there is a range of options, approaches, and alternative life styles. Effective mentors, however, do not have to be women. Men can be extremely helpful mentors, and even be more successful in some instances by opening career doors and by providing guidance to women students. While male mentors are highly desirable, they do not obviate the need for women in leadership positions (Gibbons, 1992). For women who return to graduate school after having children, day care is frequently unavailable as a part of institutional support. One can argue that the graduate school cannot be totally responsible, but as noted above, the lack of such resources inevitably affects women more than men, and can be a major factor in evoking emotional distress. Women may also return to graduate schools following a divorce, or when their children reach school age; some of them are single parents who need to juggle child care arrangements and academic pressures. More often than not, institutional flexibility is inadequate to meeting work obligations and the women are left to work out child care arrangements on their own.

FACULTY-STUDENT RELATIONSHIPS

A university is basically a hierarchical organization even though the lines of command are often subtle, complex and murky. There are roughly four general categories of "membership": students, faculty, administrative staff, and support staff. There may be "crossovers," such as graduate students with teaching responsibilities. In such a system confusion as to who has jurisdiction over whom is inevitable, and who makes academic and administrative decisions may be unclear.

Leadership may also be based on the personal characteristics and abilities of individuals who occupy specific jobs. Thus, an especially articulate faculty member within a department may wield disproportionate influence primarily by force of personality. Powerful faculty members can make decisions that run the gamut from grading of students and writing letters of recommendation to setting salaries, hiring and firing of staff and faculty, and establishing policies on which such important actions are based. Furthermore, academic faculty may be outstanding scholars but not necessarily trained in administrative tasks, and they may be surprised by difficulties inherent in the exercise of authority. On the other hand, academic scholars are as likely to be involved in the politics of self-advancement as any other group of people in a competitive environment. Thus, most graduate students at some point must confront the issue of academic politics on either the giving or receiving end. They may have jurisdiction over another person as a proctor in a dormitory or as a teaching assistant who grades students less advanced than themselves; or they may themselves be subject to the exercise of power by deans, advisors, teachers, and mentors.

Although most faculty take responsibility to their students seriously and put much time and effort into helping them to further their work, careers, and often their lives, some faculty are not so generous. Faculty can abuse their power in many ways. For instance, they can ignore students, miss or be late for appointments, neglect to grade work or fail to correct or to comment on work in progress. Such behavior can be very destructive and demoralizing for students who are left to flounder on their own. On occasion, advisors may appropriate the ideas or the work of a student to enhance their own reputations, thereby depriving the student of the credit for the idea or the research. This can happen in any field, but is probably commonest in the sciences.

In the sciences, students often do not relate to their thesis or dissertation advisors on a one-to-one basis but are part of a team that involves other graduate students. In these situations, school resembles life in a large family (Benditt, 1992). Collaborating with peers can be as supportive and as competitive as interacting with siblings. The attitude of the professor greatly influences the atmosphere in the laboratory and can have a profound effect on the student. In some laboratories, professors play favorites and the students compete for their attention. In other labs, where a more cooperative spirit predominates, the professor treats everyone in an evenhanded way, and all collaborate toward a common goal. The focus of the lab is to carry out an ongoing research program paid for by grants that the professor has obtained. Under these circumstances it is difficult to tease out the specific contributions of each participant. Indeed the notion of a Ph.D. dissertation as a separate piece of new, independent research has to be modified (Nelson, 1961).

Students, however, may have trouble accepting this model because it differs from their usual academic work which stresses originality and often discourages collaborative efforts. They may worry whether their contribution is sufficient for the Ph.D. The collaborative model also creates problems for some professors who are reluctant to let students graduate who are central to their research. Of course, there are many instances in which both student and professor value their collaboration and derive considerable satisfaction from their work together. Often the research undertaken by the student is part of a professor's ongoing project. All work done will help further the faculty member's project, and it is not always clear that the student will be able to extract results and content sufficient to form a passable dissertation. If this occurs, e.g., no dissertation is possible, it may be difficult to decide where to place the responsibility, but usually the student will suffer the greatest negative effect.

Ethical dilemmas may arise in the course of a student's work on a dissertation in collaboration with a mentor. The student may become aware that the mentor is dishonestly reporting research findings or may be plagiarizing secondary sources. This can present a difficult problem because the act of whistle-blowing can be hazardous to the student, but not reporting may cause the student considerable conflict interfering with his or her ability to work productively.

Professors are in a position to encourage or discourage students by the style and content of their comments. A faculty member can be hurtful in the ordinary course of tutoring or sometimes in the administration of oral qualifying exams. Then it is very difficult for a young person to maintain a sense of self-worth while trying to become a genuine scholar or investigator. As a result, the student may experience a substantial loss in self-confidence, not only because the teacher is realistically endowed with considerable power, but also because of an additional attribution of power by some students who experience teachers as parent substitutes.

It is a truism that grading is to some extent a subjective process so that prejudices on the part of the grader, whether they are ethnic, racist or personal toward a particular student, are always something to be guarded against. Graduate students confront this issue in their courses, either as graders or students; since grades are one key to future advancement, they matter. Even mildly critical and appropriate comments by an instructor can have a devastating effect because of the student's underlying vulnerability. Students may project an overriding sense of their total self worth onto an evaluation by an instructor whose comments are not seen simply as a reflection of the instructor's opinion of their performance in a particular area of work. The following vignette discusses the emotional crisis that somewhat surprisingly was triggered by an instructor's criticism of the work of a student:

> Rosalie, a 25-year-old fourth-year medical student, sought therapy for mild depression and discontent. She felt that her depression started after an attending physician mentioned that her recent work had not been up to its usual standard. She became upset because she was a top student in her class and proud of her superb academic performance.
>
> During the initial session with a therapist her mood was exuberant, verging on hypomania. She announced her plan to enter family practice because she liked clinical work even more than science and wanted to help people. Little else in her life had any importance apart from her work. It was apparent that Rosalie needed to impress her therapist with her devotion to work and its importance in maintaining her sense of worth. She stated that for the first time in her life she was living a long way from her parents and her much older siblings whom she missed a great deal. Her clerkships were very demanding, her social life was sparse, and she had not had time to attend church.
>
> As Rosalie became more confident of her therapist's acceptance of her, she was able to discuss another prior event. A few months before her first therapy session another student teased her about her wry sense of humor and touched her affectionately. This was enough to sweep her off her feet emotionally and somehow get her into a sexual relationship with him, knowing full well that he was engaged. As his wedding date approached, he ended the affair as tactfully as he could. She had "no regrets," but clearly felt his loss as well as that of friends, family, and church, and possibly her reputation as "the best." This rejection was an obvious blow to her self-esteem. To attempt to heal this injury, Rosalie threw herself into clinical work. This was an adaptive effort to cope with her internal distress but one which also left her very vulnerable when it did not succeed. As a result, she experienced the attending physician's criticism of her work as reflecting on her total self-worth and she became depressed.

When self-esteem is so dependent on academic achievement, any chance remark may be experienced as an assault on one's overall sense of self. Diligent academic work, while officially encouraged, can lead to social isolation and loneliness. One is vulnerable to relationships which are inappropriate in that they carry the seeds of their own defeat, and result in further discouragement and disillusion.

The misuse of power, both overt and covert, is one of the important causes of emotional problems for graduate students. Sexual harassment, which is a form of such misuse, varies all the way from inappropriate remarks and "affectionate" touching, to clear-cut sexual invitations or gestures. Students usually decide to endure abuse for fear of alienating the faculty member or being viewed as a "troublemaker." Such abuse can operate up or down the hierarchy; that is, graduate students may be subject to pressures by faculty members or may abuse their own power as teaching assistants, becoming involved, sexually or romantically, with undergraduates with whom they are in a teaching relationship.

Because the power structure in the university is sometimes less clearly defined than in many businesses or other organizations, such as the military, two individuals may begin a sexual relationship without thought as to the hierarchical implications. Such involvement may not be recognized by the participants as a boundary violation. However, where a power differential exists and one party can influence the career or record of the other negatively or positively, the situation cannot be looked on as involvement between two equal, consenting adults.

When faculty members become sexually involved with students, it is almost always destructive to the students. Given the disruption that ensues when a relationship between individuals of different rank breaks up, it is not surprising that emotional difficulties are frequent and lead to the student's need for therapy. Most universities today frown upon, if not explicitly prohibit, sexual involvements between professor and student. Universities appoint special boards to examine complaints of sexual harassment based on alleged abuse of the power differential between professor and student. These boards attempt to establish a climate that protects victims from harassment and freedom of work in academia.

Quite apart from the impact on the individuals involved, sexual interaction between professor and student can have a devastating effect on a department. A laboratory or department whose leader has an affair with a graduate student is usually fraught with intrigues and tensions that affect everybody's work. A student whose affair with a professor ends before a dissertation is completed may have great difficulty in graduating. Continued academic work with the same professor is usually impossible, leaving the student in limbo. Also, members of the department may have their own reactions to the affair and to the professor, posing grave difficulties for the student's future academic career. Even if the difficulties in the external world are ignored, sexual liaisons between students and faculty can have a devastating effect on a student's self-esteem and trust in authority figures.

Faculty members, however, may not always be the initiators of such a relationship. Students may *want* to involve professors sexually as a way of getting close to them and reducing the fear that their awe has inspired. They may feel that through sexual intimacy some knowledge will magically rub off on them. Unconsciously, they may want to become Daddy's special little child again. One female student told her therapist that she made it a point to become sexually involved with her admired professors because then she no longer felt guilty about trying to rob them of their knowledge. She paid in advance and owed them nothing further. The following vignette illustrates a typical story:

> Karen, a graduate student in history, became deeply involved, emotionally and sexually, with her advisor. Ignoring signs to the contrary, she believed that her feelings were reciprocated and that her professor would eventually divorce his disabled wife and marry her. When she returned from a prolonged research trip overseas, Karen discovered that her professor was involved with another student, that his wife was a former student and that he had an ongoing pattern of extramarital affairs. She had to acknowledge that he had no intention of leaving his wife and children. Karen was devastated. She sank into a deep depression, isolated herself in her room, unable to concentrate, think, eat or to work. Her advisor brought her to the Student Health Center saying that she was suicidal and in need of help. He implied that with this act he had discharged his obligations to her. After telling Karen that it was best if they had minimal contact with one another, he offered no solution to the dissertation problem.
>
> Psychotherapy, antidepressant medication, and a medical leave from school enabled Karen to vent her frustration and anger and to reconstitute herself. Furious at herself for being taken in by a charming and brilliant mentor, she began to understand her part in creating a fantasy of bliss with an older mentor-father whom she hoped to snatch away from his wife. Eventually she resumed her studies, found a new advisor and completed her dissertation. Nevertheless, her earlier experience had derailed her studies, alienated her from her peers, and estranged her from her family. Possibly the most unfortunate effect was a residual bitterness and mistrust of men. The goal of her therapy was limited to helping her deal with the immediate effects of her traumatic experience. When her treatment ended, she had received a Ph.D. and was assured of an academic position, but she was still wary of any intimate, committed, sexual relationships. Treatment consisted of medication for her symptoms of depression and psychotherapy to help her vent her anger and explore the nature of her relationship with the mentor. It lasted barely 12 sessions and was a good example of therapy as crisis intervention. Many issues remained unexamined, but Karen felt able to manage without any additional treatment.

Sometimes a student may misinterpret innocent remarks or behavior of a faculty member as having sexual meaning and this may lead to charges of sexual harassment. Because intent and motivation are extremely difficult to measure, both charge and denial may be almost impossible to prove. As a result of the increased awareness of possible sexual harassment, faculty members may become excessively cautious about getting close to students; unfortunately, students can thereby lose an opportunity for help and counseling. Overall, however, it behooves all members of academia to try to manage relationships so that those with power use it to benefit the younger, less established individuals with whom they work.

The unique relationship between Ph.D. students and their mentors is special and complex, combining the role of a faculty advisor with the concept of a role model (Gibbons, 1992; Moran, 1992). Understandably, the mentor becomes enormously important in the life of the graduate student, representing power, support, future success, and dreaded criticism. It is an intimate, scholarly collaboration that is focused on a highly charged intellectual pursuit. It is a student-teacher relationship with unequal power distribution. Professors have a major say about students' future careers. Students often project idealized images of their parents or their wished-for parents onto their mentors and stand in awe of the larger-than-life picture that they have created. At the same time they are often oblivious to the insecurities and conflicts of their mentors as well as to the competitiveness and envy that their own achievements may incite in the professors.

The choice of professor as mentor is influenced by both unconscious and conscious considerations. Some students are drawn to famous and widely regarded professors, and idealize them as they may have idealized a parent or parental figure; it is as if being close to a famous person confers on the students a special status, some kind of magic that affirms that they are special. Some students prefer to work with professors who give them a free hand and do not interfere too much in their work. Others, perhaps those who feel somewhat insecure and dependent, prefer professors who assign a problem and closely supervise their activities. Some students go so far as to expect professors to solve their complex equations and participate in the design of their study. Students may sometimes choose powerful and controlling mentors with whom they then become embroiled in a power struggle reminiscent of their relationship with their parents. The following vignette shows how complicated and problematic such a relationship can be:

> Sara was a 29-year-old, overweight, disheveled woman with bright, intelligent eyes behind the proverbial horn-rimmed glasses. She entered private therapy because she felt totally "stuck." During the first session of therapy she criticized her professors endlessly. She had finally found a mentor who seemed suitable, but he, too, was probably "no good." If

she did not meet the deadline for handing in her dissertation proposal, she would be out of the graduate program. Sara told the therapist that she had almost flunked out of graduate school during the first year because she missed the year-end exams. She was granted an extension by the school and later passed her exams brilliantly.

Sara's father had ridiculed her choice of graduate field but had nevertheless continued to pay for her studies. Sara worked during the first five years after college and felt happy and independent. When she realized that she needed a Ph.D. in order to succeed, she concluded that she would have to depend on her father since she felt unable to support herself. Once her father agreed, she began to resent his influence in her life. After a few therapy sessions Sara was amazed at how closely her graduate school experience resembled her home life. It became evident that her feelings toward her professor and toward her father were very similar. She experienced vacillations in their professional relationship like those with her father: a similar fear of disapproval, a wish to be admired and rivalry with the other graduate students for the professor's attention. Work in therapy helped Sara to consider the differences between her father and her mentor at least on a superficial level, and this, in turn, allowed her to take a somewhat more realistic view of the advisor and to respond more constructively in their encounters.

After several psychotherapy sessions devoted to exploring the parallels between her family and school situations, and Sara's perfectionistic tendencies, she was finally able to cobble together a proposal for her dissertation that she handed in just after the deadline. Nevertheless, it was accepted by the professor and the department. They once again made an exception for her. She felt pleased. Despite some efforts on the part of the therapist to forestall a similar pattern in therapy, Sara left treatment abruptly when the therapist refused to let her be an "exception" in regard to the agreed upon arrangements for paying her fee. All attempts at interpretation fell on deaf ears. Sara again experienced her disappointment in yet another relationship and her therapist was not able to help her understand her own role in reenacting this familiar scenario.

Sara is typical of graduate students who become enmeshed in an uncanny reenactment in the school setting of unresolved traumatic family conflicts. They attempt to rework issues of autonomy and power in a graduate school setting, and the influence of unsettled struggles with the parents spills over to their other relationships. In this instance the mentor was a shadowy figure who played his part silently, while Sara reacted to him in various ways which were determined almost exclusively by her relationship with her father.

Occasionally, students attribute to their mentor the difficulties that they are experiencing in writing their dissertation. They assume that the professor thinks poorly of them or does not take them seriously. This may sometimes represent a projection of the student's own self-criticism which then is experienced as coming from outside. Consequently the student avoids meetings with the mentor and the work stalls. If such students develop psychiatric symptoms and enter therapy, a goal of therapy may be to understand the connection between their personal problems and the difficulty in completing a dissertation. Therapeutic work is aimed at helping the student understand how internal inhibitions about work have interfered with a productive collaboration with the professor.

POSTPONEMENT ISSUES

Graduate study frequently leads to the postponement of various life events. Moving away from the family of origin, forming long-term intimate relationships including marriage and parenthood are actions that, while not impossible to combine with graduate school, may be postponed because the individual feels that they will interfere in some way with the graduate work. Thus, students may feel that one part of their life is voluntarily or involuntarily on hold in the service of obtaining a degree. They hope that the degree will open the door to the treasure house of professional competence and success; it will finally enable them to participate in the long postponed events, responsibilities, and rewards of adulthood.

Furthermore, as noted previously, these issues are not identical for women and men. Thus, if a woman wants to have a child, she must consider time in a way that a man need not. Since some programs of graduate study take a long time, women may feel pressure to complete the task early and become anxious about delays or lack of progress in their work or in their ability to find romance and marriage. Men may worry about financial dependency in graduate school and feel pressure to become independent as a way of affirming a sense of masculinity and adulthood.

Sometimes the postponement is more unconscious than deliberate. The following vignette describes a man who seems to have postponed developing the ability to function more autonomously in relation to his parents and then was confronted with the necessity of accomplishing this in a short space of time, resulting in a rather severe depression:

> Duane was a second-year graduate student in anthropology who sought therapy because of increasing depression and inability to study. He had

entered graduate school approximately 10 years after graduating from college. The events leading up to the decision and his choice of field never really became clear, except that he had held a job since college which had little or no possibility of advancement. More importantly, the decision seemed to coincide with several other developments in his life.

Duane was an only child. He had lived throughout his college and initial work period in his parents' home. Shortly before applying for graduate school he had moved into his own place and simultaneously had become involved in his first serious relationship with another man. His new independence, however, soon was threatened by the terminal illness of his father which was followed shortly by the death of his mother. Inevitably, Duane had spent considerable time providing help with their care and keeping the house going, time that basically came from his studies. After his parents' death, he inherited their house and he and his partner moved in. Duane felt that this should have been an ideal arrangement, but instead he found that he had trouble studying due to the demands of running the household. Because Duane's partner traveled quite frequently on business, he was not available to help with the house, and Duane felt quite lonely. Gradually he became increasingly dysfunctional, began using drugs more, and began to feel quite hopeless about life.

Therapy consisted of exploring the events of the immediate period of dysfunction and allowing him to express a range of feelings about his parents' death. Duane recognized that he had delayed living independently and as a result, he then felt overwhelmed about assuming responsibility for himself. When one of his therapy sessions had to be canceled, his therapist empathically understood his feelings of abandonment and anger. This experience helped him to understand more about his relationship with his partner and enabled him to be more accepting of his partner's needs for autonomy as well. An antidepressant was also prescribed and the combination of medication and psychotherapy brought him relief rather rapidly.

This vignette describes a man for whom some developmental steps were delayed. He remained quite dependent on his family of origin until his mid-thirties and had not experienced any sustained sexual intimacy until roughly the same age. Therapy helped him to develop a more mature relationship with his partner. His depression was connected with feelings of guilt related to moving away from his parents prior to their death as well as his remorse about his feelings of anger and abandonment that complicated his mourning. Therapy helped to restore his ability to function in his graduate work and to support maturation in his personal life.

FINANCIAL ISSUES

There are various ways to undertake graduate study on a part-time basis, but most students prefer, if possible, to study on a full-time basis, and sources of money then become important. There are sources within the university for loans and jobs as well as jobs that become a part of the educational program, such as teaching assistantships. In addition to the practical issue, there often are emotional components secondary to whatever solution has been reached. Some families who, without question, have helped support their children through college are unable or unwilling to help them through graduate school. For many members of the parental generation, graduate study did not seem necessary or desired, and some parents regard the pursuit of further education (perhaps correctly) as a way of avoiding looking for and finding a job. Furthermore, parents may disapprove of the student's choice of study. They may have also disapproved of the choice of major in college, but there, at least, all students graduate with a bachelor's degree. They may also view professional schools differently than Ph.D. programs. The latter may worry parents that the chosen field does not seem as promising as earning a living as law or medicine.

In addition, some parents can afford to finance their children's graduate study but feel that is in their children's best interest for them not to do so or to do so only partially. This is not necessarily a rejection of the student. It may be a way of supporting their child's autonomy and self-esteem by expecting them to contribute to the financing of their own graduate education through loans, summer jobs or savings.

The following vignette illustrates typical issues that may arise when a student stays at home for financial reasons making psychological separation from the family of origin is more difficult. The problem in this case is compounded by the attitudes of the student's parents toward graduate study:

> Lena was a 24-year-old graduate student in biology who sought treat-
> ment for episodes of recurrent anxiety and discomfort in social situa-
> tions. Although she excelled in her academic work, she was socially
> isolated and avoided dating. She felt lonely and was distressed about
> eating in front of others. Lena was an only child who lived at home
> while attending college and graduate school and she was the first per-
> son in her family to graduate from college. Her parents were somewhat
> dubious about the value of her achievement. They did not understand
> the study requirements and tended to make comments such as "why
> don't you go out and get a job rather than sitting around reading books
> all day?" She dreamed of having her own apartment but felt that she
> could not afford to as long as she remained in graduate school. She
> worried that living at home with her intrusive parents who prevented

her from dealing with her social inhibitions and having an independent life.

Lena came self-referred to the university mental health service and began psychotherapy as well as adjunctive medication to control the recurrent episodes of panic. In therapy she explored ways of maintaining privacy while remaining in her parents' home and also ways of becoming emotionally less dependent on them. She was surprised to discover that she did not have to share everything with her parents. With gentle encouragement from her therapist she began to experiment with social situations, conferences and dance classes. She gradually became optimistic that by the time of graduation she would be more at ease socially, would find a job and be able to afford to live on her own. The very idea of living alone evoked some fears initially but with continued treatment Lena's anxiety had decreased, allowing her to tackle new challenges.

This vignette illustrates how external practical problems, such as limited finances, can be used unconsciously to avoid recognizing internal conflicts about separation from the family. It also illustrates the difficulty of maintaining a positive attitude toward pursuing graduate study while living at home when the family does not comprehend what it takes to succeed in school and is not sympathetic. Lena's family criticized and found fault with her behavior, perhaps because they envied and resented Lena's achievements.

Although Lena portrayed her parents as unsupportive and even obstructive, her therapist helped her to recognize that she adhered to this view of them to avoid becoming aware of her own *internal* conflicts. Lena was conflicted about her ambition, her independence, and consequently her place in the family. In psychotherapy she was supported by her therapist as she found ways to change habitual patterns that interfered with her ability to reach her own desired life goals. The therapist maintained a stance of mild skepticism about some of Lena's self-described limitations. Rather, she was helped to explore her anxiety which interfered with her trying out new experiences. She responded to this approach with remarkable success.

This vignette further illustrates the inhibiting effect of anxiety on interpersonal relationships. The source of Lena's anxieties and their relationship to her being in graduate school context was not clarified, but it is likely that she would have been socially anxious in any setting. In her relatively brief therapy, there was no attempt to uncover or address other problems. In some ways, the most remarkable aspect of the case is that Lena could perform so well in her work.

Graduate programs provide various kinds of financial aid in the form of fellowships or teaching assistantships which are of modest help in contributing to board and lodging in addition to covering tuition; they also offer experience for future teaching or research. This aid, though helpful financially, contains conditions that put pressure on the student, such as the need to continue a program of study or forfeit the aid. Occasionally, when students are advised to take a leave of absence for emotional reasons they are unwilling to do so because it will mean loss of the living stipend. When stipends are available, however, they are often set below the poverty line. The result is that the student is more concerned about finances than about academics.

There are many different responsibilities assigned to teaching assistants (TAs). In some departments, TAs grade papers and exams and have little direct contact with students. More often, they are additionally assigned to a large introductory course, attend lectures and teach a discussion section. TAs may also perform housekeeping duties such as taking attendance, and tending to projectors and lighting. In the sciences, they also run lab sections and are also expected to maintain office hours and generally to be available to answer students' questions.

Most TAs have had no prior teaching experience or formal education courses. They teach as they were taught. Some take their responsibilities seriously and devote long hours to preparations, at times to the detriment of their own work. Others will manage to keep just one step ahead of their students. While many TAs handle their work as teachers without much difficulty, some become conflicted when faced with time pressures in their own academic work. Those TAs who feel stymied in their own work may deny the reality of their own situation and decide to devote their major energy to teaching, only to find that they have to petition for incompletes or extensions in their course work. Such delays in academic progression may result in additional financial problems for the student and increase stress on them, especially when money for stipends is limited.

Currently, there is considerable discussion in some academic circles about defining the connection of TAs to the university. On some campuses, TAs have organized and either joined an existing union or attempted to form their own union. These TAs argue that their teaching duties essentially make them employees; therefore, they qualify to be union members and to receive union benefits. The university counter-argument is that teaching responsibilities are part of TAs' academic training; therefore, their status remains as students and they are not eligible to be union members. If TAs were to join or form unions, they will clearly alter the nature of their relationship with their university. How this controversy will eventually play out and what effect it will have on the role of TAs within the university is unclear.

Another role for graduate students in need of funds is that of resident tutor or proctor in an undergraduate dormitory. Many schools offer free room and board and a stipend to graduate students willing to live in a dormitory and supervise a group of undergraduates (usually 20-40). This role is highly prized because it provides a fulfilling kind of recognition and experience; graduate students are selected for maturity, caring attitudes and interpersonal skills. Sometimes tutors go through a training program and are given some support to help them when they encounter difficulties.

The role of tutor can be taxing and draining. The graduate student may become involved with student tragedies or with illnesses, behavior disorders and other complicated situations. Often, the caring attitudes of graduate students who are attracted to this role make them vulnerable to overinvolvement in the emotional needs of undergraduates. Tutors may also be drawn into situations in which they side with undergraduates in struggles with the university's authority structure, an especially risky situation when alcohol or other drug use is involved. The following vignette illustrates how an emotionally healthy, busy graduate student with good intentions can be drawn into an inappropriate relationship with a needy undergraduate. It underscores the importance of adequate training, supervision and support for graduate students who accept the role of resident tutor:

> Mary was a medical student when she successfully competed for a position as a resident tutor in an undergraduate dormitory. The job appealed to her long-standing interests in adolescent medicine and psychiatry. She moved into a section of the dormitory that housed 36 students. Several months later a male sophomore in Mary's dormitory was accused by a female freshman of sexual harassment via e-mail messages. The young man was socially backward and eccentric. He considered his e-mail messages to be friendly overtures and he was crushed by the accusations of harassment. As his tutor, Mary reached out to him in an effort to lift his spirits, educate him socially and help him to resume his school work. She began meeting with him regularly in her room to monitor his progress.
>
> The student began talking openly with Mary about his loneliness and his longstanding problems with self-image. He soon began to seek her out with increasing frequency and it became apparent that he had developed a "crush" on her. At first, she found it rewarding to hear his unfolding story and to sense his development of trust, but when he openly confessed his feelings of love, she felt both frightened and guilty. For several weeks she struggled with the problem herself but felt that she could not extricate herself gracefully without hurting him. With an increasing sense of desperation, she sought counseling from the mental health service on campus. By then she was frightened, preoccupied, and was experiencing insomnia and difficulty concentrating.
>
> With the help of a brief course of therapy, Mary was able to see that the young man had stirred her own yearnings for closeness and had underscored her own frustrations at not being able to find a man of her

own. Her therapist enabled her to recognize that she had identified with the young man's social clumsiness and with the depths of his needs. With the therapist's help, she learned how to set appropriate limits in a tactful and considerate fashion.

Other graduate students support themselves through ancillary jobs; occasionally these jobs use the talents of the student, but most often they are fairly menial. The income from such jobs may solve their fiscal crisis, but students often find themselves exhausted physically and distracted mentally. Some students, in an effort to economize, jeopardize their health through poor diet and failure to obtain proper health care. Although most universities have student health services, their resources may be limited, and students must usually pay for medications; they may not be able to afford the prescribed medication. A more insidious effect of the lack of funds is the depressive impact of always having to watch one's pennies and consequently to eschew pleasures and indulgences. As already noted, this may be especially difficult for those who have earned money prior to returning to graduate school (Johnson and Schwartz, 1989).

Furthermore, the need to live frugally makes it difficult not to compare oneself invidiously with friends or college classmates who are already established in the professional work force. Thus, it may feel like a blow to self-esteem when graduate students note their economic poverty relative to peers, and perhaps even to chronologically younger people who are already earning large salaries and able to enjoy some of the rewards of material success.

Commercial personal loans are additional sources of funding for graduate students; their availability is directly related to the program of study. Frequently, because medical students amass such large debts, they tend to choose high paying specialties after graduation. Such large loans are probably made with the earning potential of a physician in mind and would not be available to a divinity student or an art student. Some Ph.D. students in the liberal arts manage to take out loans, but when they are ready to graduate, discover that jobs are scarce. In a few unhappy instances graduate school departments may not be truthful about employment possibilities when the students begin; in other instances the department is not dishonest, but the job market changes significantly over the five to seven year period that it takes to obtain the degree. What had been initially seen as open and promising has become closed.

The large group of students who return to graduate school after having held a job for a significant period of time may have lived relatively comfortably from a financial standpoint. Suddenly they find themselves quite pinched. They may not have adequately prepared for this change in their lifestyle and find it difficult to deal with the emotional problems that ensue. It may also make the financial consideration of planning for a secure retirement problematic, as illustrated in this vignette:

> Jacqueline was a 48-year-old single woman who came to the Health Center with symptoms of depression and difficulty finishing a dissertation in French Literature. She had left graduate school 15 years before, having been unable to finish her dissertation because of her advisor's death, which devastated her and left her quite depressed. Anyone would have been hard hit by such a death, but she was especially vulnerable. She had lost her father to cancer when she was six and, later in her life, worked hard to put herself through school and help her family financially.
>
> Jacqueline briefly attempted to cope with her depression through psychotherapy following her advisor's loss, but rather quickly decided to withdraw from school instead. She eventually found a job that gave her considerable prestige and money, but she felt that she had left something unfinished and returned to school to complete her degree. Unfortunately, a suitable advisor was not available, and the financial aid office expected her first to deplete her accumulated assets, which were earmarked for her retirement, before they would consider helping her. She found it difficult to live as a student on a very tight budget with no money for vacations and such things as occasional visits to restaurants to which she had become accustomed.
>
> In therapy she spent a surprising amount of time discussing issues of money: where she could borrow some and how much she would have left when she graduated. She complained bitterly about many of her family members who were unsympathetic and unhelpful; this reflected many old disappointments in addition to her fears of having nothing left for her retirement.
>
> In this instance, Jacqueline's return to graduate school was a conflicted choice in the context of her overall life situation. She had returned to graduate school precipitously without first carefully considering what resources would be available to her. Consequently, she experienced a self-enforced reactivation of an angry dependency on institutions and members of her family. Part of maturation involves accepting the loss of unrealized potentials and letting go of unfulfilled ambitions. In Jacqueline's case, however, there was a mixture of external problems and unresolved psychological conflicts around autonomy and dependence. The rejection of her application for financial aid did not take into account her age and her need to plan for retirement. The expectation that she deplete her retirement assets prior to being eligible for routine aid was a severe blow to Jacqueline. Realistically, it contributed to her spending inordinate amounts of time worried about money

and not being able to attend to her primary task in graduate school: writing her dissertation.

Jacqueline's psychiatrist in the health center had also seen other older students with similar problems in applying for financial aid. In her role as consultant to the administration, she suggested a review of the policy which did not take into account the realistic financial needs of older students in planning for their retirements. As a result, this practice was eventually changed.

CHANGING FIELDS

In our culture one is expected to make a clear career choice before beginning graduate study, but students often change their areas of interest while in graduate school. The notion of changing fields may arise when the work is not going well or when there is a particularly boring stretch. The feeling can be relatively evanescent or it can escalate into a full-scale obsessive crisis with no apparent solution. Obviously, the farther along the student is in a given program, the harder it is to change both practically and emotionally. Realistic reasons for changing fields include having misjudged their suitability for the actual type of work required in a particular field, such as long hours at the bench or in the library. Students may also find that total immersion into a subject is much less exciting than it seemed during a survey course in college.

Other field changes are motivated by a mixture of internal and external reality. Frequently a troubled relationship between student and faculty is the initial symptom of difficulty. Despair over ever being able to resolve the impasse may lead the student to hope that change will solve the problem. More commonly, of course, the problem recurs with a different faculty member once a change is made. The following vignette describes a student who was unhappy but uncertain as to the real cause. Therapy helped him to clarify his feelings and make a decision:

> Charles was a graduate student in chemistry who came to the health service complaining of problems in the lab where he was having particular difficulty with the chief. Charles explained that people did not speak to each other much in the lab and that his work was not appreciated. He suspected that the project he was working on would profit his professor's research grant but would not produce results sufficient to earn him a doctorate.
>
> Charles was the older of two siblings. His mother was a housewife, a quiet woman who did not try to control Charles' life. His father, who died of a difficult cancer when Charles was 17, had been a dominant,

bossy person who had ignored and belittled his gentle but able son. Charles readily acknowledged that he both worshiped and hated his father, and that he had been unable to mourn his death.

Charles was extremely astute psychologically and he asked himself an important and key question, one that usually takes some time to emerge in therapy: was his perception of the dynamics in the lab accurate, or was it colored by feelings that he carried over from his position in his family of origin? If his perception was skewed, a change to another lab would not help; if his analysis of the lab was accurate he should change labs. His therapist, of course, could not provide the answer, but listened and helped Charles in a different way.

His therapist did not want to contribute to Charles' own tendency to undermine his own autonomy in deference to an authority. In some respects, Charles was repeating this familiar pattern in his relationship with his therapist as well as in his relationship with his lab chief. His therapist helped Charles to observe this pattern instead of re-enacting it with him. In this way, Charles was able to understand an important part of his internal contribution to his problem, and was able to decide for himself how to handle his situation. Eventually he decided to move even though a move meant a lost year of school. Follow-up some years later revealed that Charles thrived in the new lab, graduated and earned a prestigious fellowship. This vignette illustrates how difficult it is to sort out the contribution of internal conflicts and external reality in a presenting problem. In this instance, Charles' conflict with his father did not necessarily distort his perception of reality in the lab. Given the opportunity to examine the situation in a supportive therapeutic setting, he reached a fruitful decision in a few sessions.

Graduate study in a Ph.D. program usually lasts from four to seven years or more. During this time, economic conditions and available jobs within a given field may change dramatically (Menand, 1996). Students who were assured of a future career may have to reexamine the possibilities in their field and consider a change in direction. By graduation the student may have already invested so much time and effort in a particular area that the prospect of change seems daunting. What seemed like a sure future must be reconsidered, causing students to feel that they made the "wrong" choice. This can lead to considerable anxiety and sometimes depression.

In recent years a national trend toward early academic retirement has led some students to question whether the lengthy time spent in graduate school is worthwhile if only a limited number of years remains to practice one's profession. Another more vexing problem for graduate students considering an academic career is the possible scarcity of tenured positions on university faculties and, if retirement pressures come earlier, tenure may be an unattainable goal. Mandatory retirement is no longer legal and the student population is no longer increasing at the same rate, but such changes and realistic uncertainty can easily lead to feelings of depression bordering on despair, especially at moments when the work is not going well. It is a mistake, then, to assume that any wish to change fields is the result of psychopathology; on the other hand, a student may benefit from talking about the situation in a therapeutic context, as Charles did.

Chapter 6:

Diversity
in the Graduate Student Population

OLDER STUDENTS

Many students do not enter graduate school immediately after college. Significant numbers of older graduate students enter graduate school later in life and find the opportunity for further education rewarding and satisfying. But some older students may find it difficult to return to student status, especially when their teachers are the same age or younger than they are (Slotnick et al., 1993; Johnson and Schwartz, 1989). Older students may have had more actual experience in a given field than the instructor and may not be shy about challenging the teacher. Some older students who resent their change in status may behave in an aggressive and difficult manner that others interpret as arrogance. A teacher who is insecure may find such encounters intolerable.

The following vignette is an example of the difficulties an older student experienced:

> Edith was a 45-year-old, married, mother of two who returned to school with the intention of obtaining a Ph.D. in sociology. Her children had reached adolescence and required less attention. She had never worked full-time but had done extensive editorial work and during her early married years produced a significant number of published scholarly works on a free-lancer basis. She expected that her teachers would acknowledge her past accomplishments and give her special consideration and respect. Instead, her teachers tended to ignore her, perhaps

[Haworth co-indexing entry note]: "Chapter 6: Diversity in the Graduate Student Population." Co-published simultaneously in *Journal of College Student Psychotherapy* (The Haworth Press, Inc.) Vol. 14, No. 2, 1999, pp. 57-70; and: *Helping Students Adapt to Graduate School: Making the Grade* (Committee on the College Student, Group for the Advancement of Psychiatry) The Haworth Press, Inc., 2000, pp. 57-70. Single or multiple copies of this article are available for a fee from The Haworth Document Delivery Service [1-800-342-9678, 9:00 a.m. - 5:00 p.m. (EST). E-mail address: getinfo@haworthpressinc.com].

because she did not appear to need any help. Her perception of neglect hurt her deeply; she became depressed, had difficulty keeping up with her work and entered therapy.

In reviewing her life history with her therapist, Edith described a childhood in which she felt her mother had focused her attention on a retarded younger sibling. Prior to her therapy, Edith had not recognized how angry she had felt about her early experiences in her family. Once she did, she began to appreciate how these feelings also influenced the way she responded to the current lack of recognition by her teachers. While she continued to have problems with her instructors, her depression became less handicapping. She began to feel more pleasure in her academic work, became less antagonistic and more productive.

This vignette illustrates the effect of encountering a situation that is at odds with one's expectations. It also demonstrates how long buried feelings can be revived unexpectedly if current circumstances happen to parallel the earlier one.

Some older students may unwittingly expect that returning to graduate school will solve problems in their life which may be unrelated to the rewards of additional education. These expectations that graduate school will be able to correct long-standing problems are, of course, unrealistic. When students bring such hopes with them and, for understandable reasons, the faculty does not appreciate these added expectations. The students may then feel that the university "owes" them something. Thus, when the university is not able to provide the "needed" resources, the students are disappointed and frustrated by the perceived failings of the system.

Older students may have commitments that interfere with their school work such as child care or attending to aging parents who require time and energy. All may go smoothly so long as everybody's health holds up, but the arrangement is so delicately balanced that even a minor upset, such as an illness of a caretaker or a sudden closure of a day care center, leads to the collapse of the entire edifice. If upsets occur repeatedly, the student may question whether school is worth the anguish.

MARRIED STUDENTS

Marriage patterns vary in the graduate school population. Both members of a couple may be at the same school but in different programs, both may be at different schools, or one of the partners may be working at a job to provide the financial support for the family unit (GAP Report, 1975). Sometimes students who are part of a couple end up in two different cities because one has finished graduate school before the other and is offered a position in another location. The stress of commuting for graduate students may not be different from those of commuting for other couples, but the impact of these difficulties may not have been anticipated or considered. Separation reactions at the end of a weekend, phobic responses, depression and loneliness can interfere with the student's performance and be a source of conflict for both partners.

Furthermore, if the couple has children, the traditional allocation of household responsibilities may be difficult to maintain. The couples' flexibility in breaking the traditional mold may be crucial to completing the program of study, not to mention the solidity of the marriage. If the husband is the student and the wife is working to earn money and, in addition, is expected to do all of the house work, she may resent the fact that he seems to be doing nothing while "he gets into the mood to work on his thesis." A divorced or unmarried parent with a child has some of the same problems that married couples do but with even less flexibility in time and less energy to cope with the problems.

The following is an example of an individual who, with the help of therapy and the opportunity to attend graduate school, was able to change what appeared to be a fixed pattern of response. It is the story of a woman who initially sought therapy because of a marital problem, but who, as she progressed in therapy, found graduate study an important element in the resolution of her difficulties:

> Pamela was a 36-year-old woman married to a somewhat authoritarian physician. She worked part-time as a physical therapist and was very involved with her two young daughters. She sought therapy because of increasing unhappiness in her marriage. The daughter of a perfectionistic and highly critical mother, Pamela had married a similarly demanding man who was accustomed to obedience in his clinic and insisted on the same at home. Everything ran on his schedules: outings, work, meals, family conferences, even sex. He chose the children's clothes and had the final say over his wife's choice of clothing and domestic purchases. Although a smart and sophisticated woman in most areas of her life, Pamela was unaware that she assumed a role in her marriage that was the same as her mother. Rather, her distress centered on her feelings of inadequacy and her inability to please her husband. Pamela chose a woman therapist although she was not conscious of the reason this was important to her.
>
> As the therapy progressed and she became aware of her powerlessness and rage, conflict and battles ensued between Pamela and her husband. These initially gave her severe misgivings; she assumed that she was at fault. In her therapy, Pamela recognized ways in which she

was repeating her earlier childhood experience with her mother in her relationship with her husband. Gradually she restored her self-esteem.

As she discovered the assertive side of herself, she decided to apply to a rigorous Ph.D. program. She was accepted and started in a timid manner. To her surprise and pleasure, she quickly began to excel. Her advisor was a competent and confident woman who admired Pamela's achievements, and soon became both mentor and friend. She was invited to participate in the mentor's extensive research undertakings and was taken aback when other students looked to her for tutoring. She was again pleasantly surprised when a dreaded course in statistics came easily to her, and she recalled her childhood interest in and ability with numbers. She changed her focus from preparation for a service career to a pursuit of hard science in academia.

At first Pamela hid her achievements from her husband, fearing that he would be angry and/or competitive with her. As time went on and her success could no longer be hidden, he actually welcomed her partnership and participation in the marriage and their relationship became a source of pleasure and cooperation to both. Such a happy outcome does not always occur because a less secure husband may feel threatened by his wife's success and assertion and be unable to tolerate the change.

This vignette illustrates the development of a woman whose emotional growth was constricted by her marital relationship in part because she had been predisposed to accepting a subservient role. Entering treatment, essentially for reasons having to do with the marriage, she developed an interest in graduate school possibly as a result of identification with a woman therapist. The fact that the student then chose a female advisor seems to indicate the importance of successful role models in establishing a satisfactory work identity. The sequence for her was marriage, children, and then graduate school. This is not an unusual pattern for women. Whether they succeed in actualizing their innate talents may depend on the "fit" in the marriage or the meshing with a particular program in graduate school. "Fit" can be as important in graduate study as it is in marriage.

MINORITY STUDENTS

Issues of diversity or multiculturism on university campuses are rife with both opportunities and challenges. Obviously, these issues affect more than graduate students, but they often affect graduate students disproportionately because of the graduate student population is more diverse; bringing together talented people with vastly differing world views and experiences can enhance the quality of education and university life. It can bridge gaps in perspective and perhaps allow for a reformulation of thoughts and ideas that can be enriching personally and for society as a whole. This ideal has relevance not only for the academic but for the civic and corporate worlds as well. Although most people embrace in theory the value of diversity, its implementation frequently raises tensions. When one contemplates the range of factors that can distinguish people, such as nationality, culture, language, race, gender, sexual orientation, physical disability, age, and class, one realizes that it would be an immense task to accommodate the needs and interests of every group.

Definitions of diversity and multiculturalism are greatly affected by political considerations. Some proponents of diversity attempt to counter "Eurocentric" practices in education by promoting other ethnocentric views, while others approach diversity by insisting that it "shun narrow particularisms, parochialisms, and separatisms, just as it rejects false universalisms" (West, 1993). The key to successful diversity programs in universities lies in addressing the psychological impact of "being different" on the individual and acknowledging histories of different groups without attempting to homogenize the groups and to substitute one mythology for another.

It is necessary to consider and understand how a sense of "differentness" affects individual identity, group identity and interpersonal processes. It is a mistake to think of group identity and individual identity as interchangeable. There is strong empirical evidence that racial identity and individual identity operate independently most of the time, and may be linked only under certain conditions (Cross, 1985). Furthermore, no one person can be identified by a single characteristic. We are members of multiple groups simultaneously, and the salience of a particular group defining characteristic depends on the social context. If one is the only physically challenged person or openly gay person, or person of color within a department, the difference may complicate ease of interaction with others who do not share the "different" characteristic and may be prejudiced toward it or simply unaware of its importance.

Some distinguishing characteristics are visible, e.g., race, physical disability, gender, while others, such as sexual orientation, religion, or nationality are less obvious and require greater familiarity to determine. Some differences confer stigma and evoke more social hostility than others. The complex interaction between an individual's sense of differentness, the visibility of the difference, and the social response to that difference influence a host of psychological processes that ultimately determine an individual's comfort or discomfort within an environment, and sense of belonging. Pinderhughes (1989) has found that a person's experience of differentness is often fraught with conflict and anxiety, irrespective of the cultural background.

Some students enter graduate and professional programs with a fairly consolidated sense of self in all its aspects, but some continue to struggle with the meaning and significance of their particular differences and have major conflicts about being different from other students. Individuals respond variously to being part of a numerical minority. Many handle it calmly and with equanimity, but some experience being categorized as a "minority" distressing. Those who are troubled may feel alienated, isolated, and displaced. Some experience frank anxiety, depression and even disorganized thinking. Because of the small size of many graduate departments, complex issues related to diversity become even more exaggerated. The following vignette illustrates some of these problems:

> Gary was a 25-year-old African-American man who was in his first year of law school at an elite university when he sought therapy for help with his "academic paralysis" and "difficulty adjusting to the structure of law school." He believed that law school was less flexible than graduate school and placed more time constraints upon him. Additionally he described sensing "racial" and "economic class" tensions between himself and his classmates.
>
> Gary was born and reared in the South. He was the oldest of three children and the only son. His mother dropped out of high school during her junior year and had worked as a seamstress in a clothing factory ever since. His father dropped out of school at the age of 12, was functionally illiterate and worked as a seasonal farm laborer. Although his parents lacked much formal education, they encouraged Gary's interest in learning and had always talked of his obtaining a college education.
>
> Gary excelled in the classroom. Upon his graduation as valedictorian of his high school, he entered an historically black college. He continued his excellent academic performance in college and decided to pursue a Ph.D. in history at the same institution. After two years of graduate study, he became interested in attending law school because of his concerns about his financial future as an academic. Having been the first person in his extended family to attend college, he felt tremendous pressure to succeed and "be a model of success."
>
> At the beginning of therapy. Gary often spoke of underlying covert race and "class" tensions between him and classmates. He noted how "white" things were at graduate school and how much this differed from college where he was surrounded by "brothers and sisters from all over the place" and where he felt more at ease socially. He described greater hesitancy to "get to know people" and found himself disclosing less information about himself and his background. He indicated that these racial and class tensions emerged primarily in the context of discussing case law, particularly in the area of affirmative action. He

felt that his white colleagues had no grasp of the true experience of ethnic minorities in the United States and, as a result, were more than willing to denigrate programs that had been designed to correct "historical wrongs." He admitted that it was difficult to sit through these discussions at times and that he sometimes felt so emotional about the topic he could not articulate his thoughts coherently. He developed acute feelings of inadequacy and under these circumstances reported feeling as if he had somehow become a "living argument" against affirmative action.

Gary was equally critical of his classmates, including other African Americans, around the issue of economic class. Again he believed that his classmates had no conception of the particular difficulties faced by people who "live in grinding poverty." As therapy progressed, race and class concerns became less prominent themes. Indeed, as the therapist guided Gary to explore his feelings about his transition from an historically black institution to a predominantly white, elite university, Gary began to talk more openly about his life long struggles to feel accepted and to belong. He acknowledged that he chose to go to an historically black college because he feared he would fail if he went to any of the predominantly white universities to which he had been accepted.

He began to talk about the growing distance between himself and his family as his life experiences expanded and as he began to feel that he had less and less in common with them. He spoke poignantly of their lack of understanding of even the basic demands of college. He described how sad it was when he realized that his father could not understand him when he tried to tell him about his dissertation. He recalled that his father had cried in his presence only once. When Gary was five, he had asked his father about the meaning of a particular word in a story that he was reading. In tears, his father confessed that he did not know what the word was, and that he could not read. He then told Gary that he had to get an education and that he "had to do it for me." Gary recalled vividly his father's sense of shame and further talked about his own shame about his own impoverished background.

Gary's therapist helped him to recognize that his intellectual discourses about race and class issues, although valid and important, served to mask other core psychological concerns and protected him from exploring much more emotionally charged issues. As the work of therapy progressed, more about Gary's internal experience emerged and led to an examination of his sense of identity, his desire for acceptance and belonging, his role as savior in his family and his struggle with differences between himself and his family. Gary began to examine how his changing life experiences had upset his relationships with his family. He could begin to emancipate himself from the burden of succeeding as an act of redeeming the family–especially his father. His understanding of these conflicts did not eliminate them and they continued to be a source of distress in his life, but he was able to overcome his work paralysis and continue with his academic career.

This vignette illustrates some of the complex interfaces between individual psychology and experience and the social environment. Many students are accustomed to being in the minority while others find themselves in the minority for the first time in their lives. This latter group may include international students and alumni of colleges that are exclusively for women or historically for African Americans. Preceding life experiences will probably determine how well one negotiates these circumstances. Sometimes, students enjoy their minority status within a department and feel threatened when another minority person is admitted. When they realize that they feel this way they may be overwhelmed with tremendous shame and guilt, become dysfunctional and require professional help.

It is important to realize that minority students may feel heavy pressure to prove that they belong. This is most likely to occur for minority students from groups that are the most stigmatized in our society. Such pressures and the associated anxieties may have a negative effect on a student's proficiency. The burden of disproving stereotypes leads to a kind of "spotlight anxiety" (Cross, 1995) that does not afford the person the luxury of making even occasional mistakes. The degree to which persons feel that they belong has a significant impact on their relationships with other students and with those in authority.

Many students are comfortable in their sense of belonging to the university and are not reluctant to raise group related concerns; others are intimidated and fear that discussing specific discriminations would invite hostility from the larger group and lead to being made a scapegoat or labeled a troublemaker or being called "hypersensitive." Some students cope with feelings of vulnerability and powerlessness by becoming suspicious of others; they may engage in persistent conflict with those unlike themselves and find fault in the behavior of anyone who is not a member of their group. Being different can become a political issue that is injected into any discourse.

Universities are not immune from the same influences of bias and prejudice that exist in the society at large. Although it is impossible for a university to address the concerns of every numerical minority, it can work toward promoting an atmosphere of respect for the characteristics that differentiate people, while simultaneously encouraging exploration of shared characteristics. Full appreciation of diversity means realizing that human beings are complex and not reducible to simple categorization (Pinderhughes, 1989).

INTERNATIONAL STUDENTS

International students lose their usual support network when they leave their homes for a foreign country. The resulting isolation magnifies and modifies the expected problems of graduate students (Reifler, 1988; Martinez et al., 1989). The rapidly increasing number of international students in the U.S. made it increasingly urgent to provide them with appropriate support and understanding.

Some students come from European countries which have always traditionally been a source of graduate students and some, frequently on government fellowships, come from South America, Africa, India, and East Asia. Moreover, with the recent political change in previously communist countries and the opening up of China, there are increasing numbers of graduate students from eastern Europe and mainland China. Some of these students may have been offered only one opportunity for overseas academic study which adds greatly to their urgency to succeed.

International graduate students are of every age, ethnicity, and economic background. Their level of educational preparedness may vary considerably. They speak different languages and do not necessarily share basic cultural mandates. Thus, they present a diverse appearance, but internally they share more psychological struggles than one might imagine. Suppose that students from Mauritius, Portugal, Eastern Europe, Costa Rica and the southern United States–all bright, well-read, socially and academically prepared–were brought together in graduate school. Such a diverse population is very complex, and one could imagine this rich admixture of ideas, personalities, and cultures would lead to collegial discourse and debate, but this is not always the case. By its very organization, graduate school incorporates a series of values that are quite essential, if not necessarily explicit. Students often report that regardless of the differences between departments there is the same requirement: namely that all must "buy into" to a certain research paradigm based on "Western" patriarchal models and belief systems. This paradigm, whether intentional or not, is sometimes demeaning or even discriminatory toward women and students from minority cultures. Most graduate students are not consciously aware of these issues, but they nevertheless may be affected by them and experience internal struggle and confusion about the need to adapt.

Typically, the first conflicts that foreign students experience engender doubts about the wisdom of their decision to leave home and come to the U.S. for study. Sometimes the decision to study abroad has been made by their family and not by them. In that case the student may lack the enthusiasm and persistence necessary to adapt to the new country. Some students do not come to the U.S. primarily to study but to immigrate and then send for their family. Whether self-imposed or dictated by the family, this task places a considerable burden on the student. It is not easy to become a U.S. citizen. If students fail in this mission, they may feel considerable guilt and loss of self-esteem. The following is an example of a student who struggled with such a task assigned by his family:

> Vijay was an Indian student whose parents asked him to marry a U.S. citizen of Indian descent so that he could become a citizen and enable the rest of the family to immigrate to the United States. Vijay spent weekends in different U.S. cities trying to meet eligible Indian-American citizens. He did not like any of the women that he met and became quite depressed looking for a wife that he did not really want to find. He was too guilty, however, to give up the quest since this was the real reason his parents sent him to graduate study.
>
> During therapy Vijay realized that he was not ready to marry and that he still had several years of graduate study to complete. He told his parents that he decided to postpone marriage and to concentrate on his studies. His depression lifted and he was able to work better and relax more.

Myriad cultural issues face international students on arrival. Their ability to negotiate them depends partly on their country of origin and their place within the social structure of that country. Students from non-English speaking countries may have greater than expected difficulties with the language and consequently feel less competent and more isolated than other students. Furthermore, if international students are teaching assistants, undergraduates do not hesitate to complain about their language skills.

The alienation that international students experience is magnified by cultural differences. For example, a woman student from Pakistan is not accustomed to having physical contact (even shaking hands) with men. She will find it difficult to accept a friendly hug from an American student, even though she understands that it is well intentioned. Similar cultural differences make it difficult for her to find close friends among U.S. students. In addition, cultural barriers may prevent international students from associating with others even from their own country. The caste system in India, for instance, is a barrier both to needed support and friendship. Similar social barriers hinder the association of East Asian groups so that Japanese, Chinese or Korean students may feel quite isolated from one another. Different subgroups are wary or even hostile toward each other. U.S. students tend to dismiss or not recognize the presence of such class and caste incompatibilities. Even the location of the university may affect social interaction. Large cities have organized Indian communities that reach out actively to Indian graduate students; African students may find a city community more accepting of racial diversity than small, rural towns.

Cultural differences can emerge in the educational setting as well. The professor-student relationship is different in various cultures. Puerto Rican students come from a country with a collegial, relaxed sociability between professors and students, and they tend to find the U.S. attitude cold and distant. On the other hand, students from Great Britain may find the U.S. graduate school too informal, and they may have trouble finding the appropriate distance between themselves and their professors. Differing cultural norms may lead a student to a misinterpretation of the nature of the relationship with a particular professor. Some students may interpret a professor's informality as a romantic interest.

International students display signs and symptoms of emotional difficulties in ways that are culture-specific. Different cultures place different values on obedience and deference to parents and to the prerogative of the male head of the family. Thus, physical violence within marriage is not necessarily considered unacceptable. In some countries, corporal punishment of children is an accepted part of the culture. Students may come to question their traditional values as a result of living in the U.S.; wives of students raised in cultures that condone oppression of women may begin to question their roles, and thereby experience conflict and inner turmoil leading to marital difficulties.

The following vignettes illustrate a variety of difficulties that caused distress and led international students to seek therapy even though the act of seeking therapy for some is a violation of their cultural norms. Sometimes, such students first develop somatic symptoms and are referred for psychiatric treatment by their family practitioner or internist when such physicians find no physical basis for their symptoms.

> Lee was a student from the People's Republic of China whose parents, still living in China, had arranged for him to marry a woman in China when he returned home from his graduate studies. While in the U.S., however, Lee had fallen in love and developed a serious relationship with a Chinese-American woman. Lee felt torn between his personal inclinations, supported by the U.S. culture, and his duty to his parents and the Chinese tradition, which dictated that he terminate the relationship. He feared that his family would disown him if he married the American woman, and that if he ever returned to China, it would be unacceptable for him to bring along an American wife.
>
> In his sessions with his therapist, Lee explored his feelings about his conflict and was helped to feel less critical of himself about his struggle. In time, he was able to discuss his feelings with his girlfriend. With her support he told his parents; although they were not happy with the situation, they did not disown him. Their reaction enabled him to tolerate his confusion and uncertainty without making an abrupt deci-

sion. He decided to wait and see how the relationship developed and did not feel the need for further therapy.

Students who are far from home worry about what is happening to their family at home. If a family member becomes ill, students become concerned and may feel very guilty about not helping out. The following vignette illustrates this point:

> Dirk, a European graduate student, was in his first year of study abroad. When his father, who had a history of mental illness, made a serious suicide attempt, Dirk became quite upset. He felt strongly that he should leave school for a month and return to his country to meet with his father's doctors and help plan for his father's rehabilitation. Dirk's worries about his father interfered greatly with his graduate work; he was overwhelmed by trying to manage both his life and his father's illness. Dirk was seen briefly at the mental health service after referral by a faculty advisor who thought medication might be helpful. His therapist took a rather practical approach, supporting the idea of a leave to return home, which the student arranged. During the leave Dirk obtained a more realistic view of his father's situation and recognized that he could not help directly. This allowed him to pursue his studies with somewhat less interference.

Some relationships that are more readily accepted in the U.S. than in the home country as the following vignette illustrates:

> John came to the conclusion that he was gay after considerable inner struggle and succeeded in establishing a committed, satisfying long-term relationship with a partner. Toward the end of his graduate work, he became anxious in anticipation of a return to his home country where homosexual relationships were not acceptable. While his partner was willing and able to accompany him to his native land, John worried that their relationship would be considered deviant and that they would not be able to be themselves. For various practical reasons, John could not stay in the U.S. and his anxiety remained unresolved. He consulted a therapist and, after some discussion, decided to return home alone for an exploratory visit. While there he was able to find, to his surprise, a city with a gay community where he and his partner could feel comfortable.

Sometimes a family consultation seems indicated. Naturally it is much more difficult to arrange with a family living overseas and telephone calls do not permit the same ease of communication as face-to-face discussions. The following vignette is an example of a successful resolution of a conflict through a family meeting:

> Ernst, a German student was sent to the United States for graduate work in engineering because his parents thought that engineering was an appropriately practical field. In the U.S. Ernst developed an interest in theoretical physics. He wanted to change fields but feared that his family would disapprove and be disappointed if he returned home without a practical degree. His distress and anxiety were such that his advisor referred him to the campus mental health service for help. Ernst was reluctant to discuss the change in his interests with his family over the phone and planned to defer the conversation until his next trip home, a good nine months away. He had lost all interest in engineering and, consequently, could not study for the rest of the year. With the encouragement of his therapist, Ernst eventually raised the subject with his parents. The parents were upset but responded by arranging to have his mother fly in from Germany to spend two weeks with him and talk about it. During the two weeks, Ernst discussed his situation with his mother alone and in family meetings with the therapist. The parents agreed to the change in field provided that he was capable of doing the work. Once his parents agreed, Ernst felt free to look clearly at his interest and abilities in physics, and to make the change.

While this case had a satisfactory outcome, obviously not many international student families would have the time or the means to come to the United States.

Many international students have difficulty consolidating their identity. It is especially difficult for international born students to resolve issues of separation from family and home. International students frequently feel isolated and lonely. These feelings tend to interfere significantly with the process of separation because they invoke idealized fantasies of the warmth and support of home. Students who at home were busy with their own differentiation issues would not have missed the family. Once in the United States they are surprised and possibly discouraged when they find themselves missing their parents, their friends, and often their siblings.

International students may also have idealized notions of the educational or social life in the U.S. They become disillusioned when they confront the reality of student life. They may have been among the elite in their native country and find their social status greatly reduced in the U.S. They may find that other students are neither as friendly and understanding as they had anticipated nor as intellectually disciplined as they had imagined. Sometimes students leave their home country precisely in order to escape personal or family problems there, hoping that these problems will disappear in the new country. When the same kinds of difficulties arise in the new environment, they can be very disappointed and distressed. Such an experience can lead to a significant depression. Furthermore, when students encounter greater freedom in the United States than in their home country, they may overreact and require more self-discipline than at home.

Many international students encounter racial and ethnic prejudice in the U.S., something they had never felt in their own or other countries. They find it distressing and humiliating that they are perceived as stereotypes associated with their country of origin and, at times of political crises when their country and the United States are at odds, they may be greeted with hostility by U.S. students. For example, at the time of the bombing of the World Trade Center in New York City, there was strong feeling against people of Arab descent; similarly, the conflict in the former Yugoslavia evoked strong anti-Serbian feeling. Students who may have felt relatively well accepted by their peers prior to a war may find themselves shunned and excluded after the war begins.

Students' visa status can have a significant impact on their experience as graduate students. Most come to the U.S. on student visas, although some enter as exchange visitors. Those who are on student visas are not permitted to work and cannot take long university vacations. Nor can they take a leave of absence or withdraw from school for more than a few months without loss of their student visa which would force them to return home. Some students, for various reasons, feel apprehensive about going home on vacation, worrying that they will not be able to return to the U.S. Students with an emotional illness might well benefit from time away from school, but with the threat of losing their visa they will not ask for a medical leave and will struggle to stay in school until their symptoms increase to the point that they are forced to return home. This problem is not limited to graduate students, but poses a problem to all international students. In certain cultures loss of "face" is so important that a decision to return home without completing the program places a high stress on the student irrespective of the cause of the return.

International students must not only become fluent in a new language and adapt to new customs, but also face severe financial limitations. Many international students receive fellowship aid, but many options are foreclosed by money considerations. It may be financially impossible for them to go home when they receive news of illness or other anxiety-producing events, and they are left to worry, feeling helpless and guilty at not being able to help their family at home.

Chapter 7:

Psychiatric Disorders

Graduate students are as prone to serious mental illness as other adults of similar age. In a student health service one encounters bipolar, i.e., manic-depressive disorder, major depression, schizophrenia, eating disorder, obsessive-compulsive disorder (OCD), attention deficit disorder, learning disabilities and panic disorder (Arnstein, 1989). These illnesses tend to run their course, and it may be difficult to manage the more severe forms of them while an individual remains in school, depending to some extent on the availability of appropriate supports. While attending graduate school does not pose a special risk for the development of a psychiatric disorder, the stresses involved may precipitate an episode as it would in other life situations.

The milder forms of anxiety or OCD do not necessarily interfere with academic progress although they may be disabling during times of severe stress. Unlike the more severe illnesses, they rarely require hospitalization or withdrawal from the university (Pinkerton and Rockwell, 1994). Learning disabilities may persist into adulthood and graduate students with Attention Deficit Disorders (ADD) may require special help. Student Health Services should provide resources for the diagnosis of ADD (or make referrals for this service) so that appropriate assistance can be provided for such students.

Students in the throes of a manic or psychotic episode can be disruptive to the community. Their actions may become unpredictable and their altered behavior is bewildering and anxiety-provoking to those around them. Loud, pressured and intrusive manic speech is disruptive to departmental functions. Suicidal threats or acts are upsetting, all the more so in a community of students, many of whom harbor depressive thoughts of their own.

Early recognition of serious illness is extremely important. An ideal not

[Haworth co-indexing entry note]: "Chapter 7: Psychiatric Disorders." Co-published simultaneously in *Journal of College Student Psychotherapy* (The Haworth Press, Inc.) Vol. 14, No. 2, 1999, pp. 71-77; and: *Helping Students Adapt to Graduate School: Making the Grade* (Committee on the College Student, Group for the Advancement of Psychiatry) The Haworth Press, Inc., 2000, pp. 71-77. Single or multiple copies of this article are available for a fee from The Haworth Document Delivery Service [1-800-342-9678, 9:00 a.m. - 5:00 p.m. (EST). E-mail address: getinfo@haworthpressinc.com].

often realized is to have a close liaison between a psychiatrist based on campus and key university personnel–deans, resident hall advisors and coaches–who can be alerted to the signs and symptoms of a student's impending decompensation. When such a liaison can be developed, leading to a prompt referral, and when the student mental health service can respond immediately with a rapid evaluation, there is an enhanced likelihood that the psychotic episode can be contained or even averted. Several well tolerated, effective medications are now available for the treatment of schizophrenia and manic-depressive illness. These drugs make it possible for many students who might otherwise be crippled by their disease to function sufficiently well to avoid hospitalization.

Student Health psychiatrists have come to understand that a part of their work in treating the decompensating student is to help others involved with the student to cope with their own reactions, bearing in mind the need to preserve their student-patient's confidentiality. It is obvious, however, that such a system is more feasible with undergraduates. Graduate students most often live off campus, have little contact with deans and none with coaches. Because graduate students often change lodging there may not even be accurate knowledge of their whereabouts.

PSYCHOTIC ILLNESSES

A small number of graduate students will exhibit flagrant psychotic episodes. If they cooperate, comply with their medications, come regularly for their appointments and have adequate personal support, they can experience a fairly prompt remission of their symptoms. They can even complete their academic requirements if their programs are flexible enough to permit them extensions to make up missed assignments and if the student does not have fixed teaching commitments.

International students who become psychotic are a particularly difficult therapeutic challenge for the campus psychiatrist. Many are on student visas that mandate deportation if the student is hospitalized or takes a leave of absence. This reality complicates clinical decisions and adds an additional pressure to manage the problem on an outpatient basis. Concerns for the student's own safety and that of others may necessitate hospitalization.

A major mental illness has a profound effect on graduate studies. Students may be emotionally paralyzed and unable to function academically during periods of depression. As their performance deteriorates, their standing in the department drops and the department's objective negative evaluation of their work lowers their self esteem and deepens their depression. During a manic episode, what the student experiences as a creative burst may lead to nonsensical production and exhaustion which again can hurt the student's reputation and certainly stand in the way of regular progression. Students may become discouraged from making sustained efforts in school as the instability of their mood becomes apparent. Fortunately, some graduate departments are able to tolerate a wide range of devian behavior, accept the aberrations of talented students and help them to graduate.

> Frank, a 29-year-old biology student, required two hospitalizations for manic episodes during six years of graduate study. Each episode was preceded by several weeks of escalating excitement, hyperactivity, talkativeness, intrusiveness and accusatory behavior. Prior to his last hospitalization, Frank abruptly shoved a student to the ground without apparent provocation, interrupted a guest speaker and harangued the audience with stories of corruption in the university administration. Ordinarily, Frank's mania was well controlled on medication and he functioned as a respected member of a laboratory team.
>
> Before each decompensation, however, Frank skipped his sessions with his psychiatrist, reduced his medication, falsely believing that it was causing his depression. After his second hospitalization, his fellow students refused to work with him in the laboratory and appealed to the chairman of his department to remove him from school. The chairman did not pressure Frank to leave but instead suggested that he resume his sessions with his psychiatrist, which he agreed to do. He encouraged Frank to meet with the other students and reassure them that he was resuming his treatment. Despite the support within his department, Frank felt increasingly isolated and alienated. He began taking his medication and met with his psychiatrist with whom he discussed ways he could function under less pressure. Frank decided to leave the doctoral program and planned another less demanding program in biology which would lead to a master's degree instead.

This case illustrates the fragility of patients with manic-depressive illness and the effects of the student's disruptive behavior on others. The support of Frank's department head enabled him to continue in treatment and, with his psychiatrist's help, made it possible for him to redefine his career goal in a more realistic manner. This outcome was less damaging for Frank than if he had been simply forced to withdraw.

Occasionally the school is faced with an ethical dilemma: should medical students who are subject to recurrent bipolar episodes, during which they demonstrate serious defects in their professional judgment, be allowed to graduate as clinicians? Should such students be advised to pursue a medical subspecialty with little direct contact with patients, such as pathology or radiology? Should they be encouraged to go into research if they have the ability for it? These are very difficult questions that involve dealing with personal and professional rights as well as with laws relating to disability. Sometimes they raise the specter of liability actions against the school or individual faculty or staff members in the school.

The very fact that students have been treated at the mental health service is, of course, confidential and protection of this confidentiality is a matter of major concern to students. Any breaches of confidentiality can haunt a service for months, if not years. Despite every effort to protect confidentiality, important facts about the behavior of a disturbed student may be well known to the university community. A student's psychotic episode is usually "public" in the sense that other students and faculty know that the student is upset, and often question the campus psychiatrist. Except in very unusual circumstances when the situation is life-threatening, confidentiality must be maintained, preventing the psychiatrist from revealing information without student consent. Eliciting the consent of the student enables the treating psychiatrist to work collaboratively with administrators and faculty in managing the episode. It is important to try to obtain the student's permission by explaining the advantages that result from such collaboration. The psychiatrist can also be explicit about the drawbacks of "stonewalling," a stance that sometimes tends to engender anger and lack of cooperation. However, without permission freely given, a psychiatrist cannot divulge information about a patient to anyone except in certain specific situations. When a student seriously threatens suicide, a therapist appropriately needs to enlist the help of family or other agencies to hospitalize the student. It is preferable if the patient agrees and cooperates with this decision, but there are times when it may be necessary for the therapist to take action without the student's consent.

The responsibility of psychiatrists to keep their patients' confidences may sometimes conflict with their responsibility to protect the community at large (American Psychiatric Association, 1987). In many states, laws have been enacted which require psychiatrists and other physicians to report cases of actual and suspected child abuse to appropriate authorities. For psychiatrists, the most perplexing area of conflict between their obligation to their patients and to society involves what has come to be called the Tarasoff doctrine, following a California case decided in 1974 (VandeCreek and Knapp, 1983). This case established a legal precedent for psychiatrists being responsible to take steps to protect persons whom their patients seriously threaten with harm. The appropriate legal, ethical and clinical considerations involved in managing such situations are very complicated and generally warrant professional and legal consultation.

Student patients have the right to expect the same privacy from a health service as they would from any physician or clinic. The institution in the long run benefits from this strict confidentiality. The use of a student health service depends on the confidence the student body has in the strict maintenance of confidentiality. If the health service has a reputation for breaching this, except in the unusual circumstances described above, it would become next to impossible to encourage students to avail themselves of this service.

SUBSTANCE ABUSE

The situation is considerably more complicated if a student comes to the mental health service with a problem of substance abuse which apparently is not known to the school authorities. It is especially problematic if it appears that outpatient therapy is not going to be sufficient to cope with the problem. The therapist will, of course, attempt to encourage the patient to disclose what needs to be disclosed, but if that is not possible as may be the case in emergency situations, the consequences for the student may be far-reaching. Questions may be raised about the student's suitability to continue in the program.

Alcohol and other drugs abound on campus. Graduate students, like undergraduates, engage in substance abuse. It might be assumed that admission to graduate school, which requires considerable achievement, would preclude substance abuse problems, but this is not the case. Moreover, because graduate students are older, they are more likely to have developed chronic problems with alcohol. A student may have had episodes of severe intoxication earlier in life, but not have begun to drink consistently until later.

Furthermore, graduate programs have flexible work hours so that it is possible to go on a binge for a considerable length of time without anyone noticing or becoming concerned. However, when the work becomes so demanding that it is no longer compatible with heavy drinking, someone who managed to get by in college may no longer be able to manage the addiction and will need treatment. The reasons for developing serious substance abuse problems are complex and may result from a combination of biologic vulnerabilities, individual proclivities, institutional factors and the relative isolation that graduate study engenders. A full discussion of substance abuse treatment is beyond the scope of this report. It is important that university mental health services be able to assess substance abuse and make referrals to specific treatment programs in the community.

PERSONALITY DISORDERS

In addition to the episodic major disorders, there are a variety of personality disorders encountered in the graduate student population. These disorders are not necessarily different in students than in non-students, but the student context creates some specific problems. When such students are disruptive in class or in a dormitory, it may be necessary to take steps to protect the rights of other students as well as to offer therapy directly to afflicted students.

An administrative dilemma that frequently arises if therapy is provided at a university health center is whether to record diagnoses. On the one hand, offering a careful evaluation leading to a tentative diagnosis is an expected medical practice. It is also required by various accrediting bodies that may be involved if the university health service is seeking certification by a national organization. On the other hand, since many graduate and undergraduate students are still in the process of development, an accurate diagnosis may be difficult to make, and an erroneous diagnosis may have serious consequences for their futures. Prospective employers may request information from the health service, and, if the latter's policy is to honor such requests with the student's permission, there is a danger that the organization may seriously misinterpret the response.

There is also a question of confidentiality and the inhibiting effect of the possibility that the information disclosed during presumably closed sessions could be eventually released. Some health services have recommended that no information be released about prior therapy, but there are legal problems involved having to do with who has the right to determine access to information in the medical record. In most instances students have that right, and they will be likely to exercise it if a future job opportunity requires disclosure of past treatment. When students feel uncertain about maintenance of confidentiality in a student health service they will not feel safe to disclose certain kinds of information about themselves that might be quite important, and thus their therapy will be hindered.

SUICIDE

Suicide in the college and university student population has been quite thoroughly investigated; yet despite this effort, the search for definitive conclusions regarding suicide rates and predisposing factors remains incomplete. Early research findings raised the concern that university students are at an increased risk for suicide. These reports were subsequently challenged by others showing lower rates of suicide than in age and gender matched controls. These conflicting results have generated a fair amount of confusion and have prompted several reviews of the student suicide literature in past years. Most recently, Silverman (1993) analyzed all English-language studies (international and U.S.) on suicide in the "campus student" population. He concluded that only four out of 21 single site studies showed a higher rate of suicide than age and sex matched controls; the remainder of all the studies surveyed supported a conclusion of equivalent or lower rates of suicide in this population. Silverman cautions, however, that it is quite difficult to evaluate the data from all the studies done to date because of widely varying methodologies and populations. He asserts that there are very few rigorous studies which focus on student suicides as well as very few multi-site controlled studies. These deficiencies significantly limit the reliability of any conclusions that can be drawn from available data. Given these constraints, it is not possible to make conclusive statements regarding the relative risk of suicide in the graduate student population in particular. Certain predisposing factors (male gender, prior attempts, psychiatric diagnosis, substance abuse, etc.) may hold for graduate students as well as the population overall but await further clarification from further research. For now it is reasonable to encourage awareness of the risk of suicide in this population among a variety of individuals ranging from deans to peer counselors and to make mental health services as accessible and well advertised as possible (Arnstein, 1986).

Chapter 8:

Provision of Treatment

Therapy with graduate students differs significantly from that with undergraduates in that many of the characteristics of graduate students are those of adults rather than adolescents. Currently, graduate students are older generally than the 22- to 28-year age range common just two decades ago. By the time graduate students come to school, they have usually completed many of the developmental tasks of late adolescence and young adulthood, but since they are students many of the decisions about the future are still open, or have been reopened. Furthermore, many graduate students need to resolve resurfaced developmental issues. Thus, a therapist working with a graduate student needs to maintain a developmental perspective in order to understand the symptoms and difficulties that emerge at this particular time.

It is important to evaluate graduate students carefully because they tend to have more entrenched problems. Since most psychotherapy offered on campus is limited, one needs to select a focus for short term therapy or refer for longer term therapy if it is indicated and a referral is available. In some instances therapy takes the form of an extended evaluation with the aim of immediate relief of symptoms; it can also prepare a student for more extensive therapy later in life when such an option may be economically possible.

Recent economic pressures have led to the increasing popularity of brief treatment methods, such as behavior modification, cognitive therapy, and other short term psychotherapy (GAP Report, 1990). Group methods have also become more prevalent, ranging from traditional group therapy to single issue support groups such as for eating disorders or bereavement. The relatively recent introduction of new antidepressant, antianxiety and antipsychotic medications with fewer side effects permit effective pharmacotherapy and symptom relief for selected students. A combination of psychotherapy and medication may be the treatment of choice for students presenting with fairly

[Haworth co-indexing entry note]: "Chapter 8: Provision of Treatment." Co-published simultaneously in *Journal of College Student Psychotherapy* (The Haworth Press, Inc.) Vol. 14, No. 2, 1999, pp. 79-81; and: *Helping Students Adapt to Graduate School: Making the Grade* (Committee on the College Student, Group for the Advancement of Psychiatry) The Haworth Press, Inc., 2000, pp. 79-81. Single or multiple copies of this article are available for a fee from The Haworth Document Delivery Service [1-800-342-9678, 9:00 a.m. - 5:00 p.m. (EST). E-mail address: getinfo@haworthpressinc.com].

severe dysfunction. For example, a student with performance anxiety might receive careful medical and psychiatric evaluation followed by judicious use of a medication (such as a beta blocker) and psychotherapy that is focused on helping the student reduce anticipatory anxiety and facilitate success.

As the number and variety of drugs increases, psychopharmacology becomes ever more complex. Psychiatrists must learn about drug interactions and the effect of drugs on different individuals and in different age groups, and so prescribing appropriate medications is no longer a simple procedure. While drugs have numerous side effects that limit their use, they can also be extraordinarily beneficial when appropriately used for specific patients. Medications are combined in a variety of ways and since they require time to reach their maximum effect, the treatment of a depression, for example, may be lengthy and complex. There is some evidence that combining medication and psychotherapy is more effective than either alone particularly in the treatment of patients with more severe depression (Weissman et al., 1995). Also, controlling or reducing symptoms with medications enables the individual to deal with psychological problems and work more effectively in psychotherapy.

Our clinical experience has led us to believe that graduate students seek therapy at university mental health services more often than undergraduates, and therefore would be seen at a higher rate than undergraduates. It is our impression that graduate students tend to be more knowledgeable about the possible benefits of therapy, may be less concerned about the stigma sometimes ascribed to being in therapy, and make more use of mental health services. They may have experienced recurrences of earlier difficulties and realize that problems do not disappear simply as a result of the passage of time or of additional life experience. Furthermore, they may be at the point of making decisions that will affect their entire future life and recognize the usefulness of therapy at such crucial moments. We feel that graduate students tend to spend more time in therapy than undergraduates because their response patterns are relatively more fixed and their problems are less likely to respond to brief therapeutic interventions.

Those services that report seeing fewer graduate than undergraduate students may not publicize the availability of services adequately. Graduate students who are not as well connected with the informal campus network as undergraduates, may be less aware that consultation and therapy are available to them on campus. It also appears that students in some professional schools, such as law and medicine, are realistically concerned about the impact that any revelation about their being in therapy may have on their future careers, especially if they are harboring political ambitions. Some students may decide to avoid therapy altogether or to seek it privately off-campus in the hope that their confidentiality will be better served.

The concern of students about possible difficulties that may ensue if they have been in therapy is not imaginary. Some states ask questions about prior therapy on applications for residencies, medical licenses and the bar examination, placing the applicant in a difficult situation. Applicants can be truthful and risk rejection or deny that they have been in therapy and rely on the confidentiality policies of universities not to release medical information without their consent. However, the mere existence of such questions on applications creates an ethical dilemma for students who must choose to protect themselves by lying or risk the consequences of revealing information which may be misinterpreted.

If the applicant consents to the release of psychiatric information, further problems can ensue. Agencies differ in the nature of the information they require. If a diagnosis is supplied, it may result in the student not being hired and being stigmatized long after the problem has been resolved. For example, a histrionic upset young woman in crisis can initially impress an evaluator or therapist as "borderline," a "negative" diagnosis which can color a future therapist's relationship to her. The following example is unusual but describes what can happen:

> Jeffrey, a graduate student in psychology, consulted the student health service because of anxiety following the break up of his relationship with another student. He was surprised to learn that his medical records contained information about an earlier visit which he had forgotten. The son of faculty members of this same university, Jeffrey was seen at the health service when he was 10 years old. Following his parent's divorce at that time, Jeffrey had become socially withdrawn and had several sessions with a child psychiatrist who described him as "possibly schizoid." Jeffrey recovered from the reaction to the family crisis and showed no further schizoid behavior. Having become a graduate student with an exemplary record, he was chagrined that the earlier diagnosis was still attributed to him in his records. Although no negative consequences actually occurred, the student was understandably upset because it was not considered possible to expunge the diagnosis.

Some services keep mental health records separate from the general medical record and destroy the mental health records after a specified period of inactivity. This policy, adopted for a variety of reasons, would have resolved the issue in this instance. However, there are legal requirements for retaining medical records for specified periods of time which varies from state to state.

Some university health services do not release records when the request for information is to be used for administrative rather than therapeutic purposes. A form letter is sent explaining the nature of the clinic and the rationale for not releasing specific information. Most agencies accept this policy without adverse consequences to the student.

Chapter 9:

Degree or Not Degree

A Ph.D. program is a difficult undertaking and students may come up with "good" reasons to abandon the effort. A decision to leave may represent a healthy reevaluation of the student's life situation and reflect maturation and growth; on the other hand, leaving graduate school may express unresolved anxieties associated with success and achievement (Menand, 1996) The temptation to leave is especially strong at the time of choosing a dissertation topic, starting to write, or toward the end of the dissertation.

Completing the dissertation can become such a hurdle that the acronym ABD (All But Dissertation) has arisen to describe the academic status of these students. Some students may eventually settle for an M. Phil., a degree given by certain universities that formally reflects the ABD status on the way to a Ph.D. (Bertocci et al., 1992). Students do not necessarily regard ABD status as a plight; they may prefer to work part-time, gaining experience in their field and supplementing their income while completing their dissertation.

A woman may choose to start a family as an acceptable way out of graduate school. One woman gave up in mid-course to have a baby rather than wrestle with finding a dissertation topic. She felt ill-prepared and inadequate to the task despite clear evidence of superior ability (Gold, 1978). Since men cannot become pregnant to justify withdrawing, they find other socially acceptable reasons for leaving graduate school. We do not know whether more women than men drop out of graduate school.

Stresses impinge on men and women differently, and it is not clear which factor or combination of factors is more likely to lead to completion of graduate school. Some families are willing financially to support sons but not daughters, which conveys a strong message in addition to the actual aid. In

[Haworth co-indexing entry note]: "Chapter 9: Degree or Not Degree." Co-published simultaneously in *Journal of College Student Psychotherapy* (The Haworth Press, Inc.) Vol. 14, No. 2, 1999, pp. 83-85; and: *Helping Students Adapt to Graduate School: Making the Grade* (Committee on the College Student, Group for the Advancement of Psychiatry) The Haworth Press, Inc., 2000, pp. 83-85. Single or multiple copies of this article are available for a fee from The Haworth Document Delivery Service [1-800-342-9678, 9:00 a.m. - 5:00 p.m. (EST). E-mail address: getinfo@haworthpressinc.com].

our society there is a tacit expectation that men will wish to ascend to the top ranks, and women will remain in supportive positions (Barinaga, 1992; Benditt, 1992; Healy, 1992). Thus, there may be less support for an ambitious woman than for an ambitious man. Many women graduate students struggle with conflicts over whether they deserve the degree and whether it is congruent with their femininity. When the struggle is unconscious, they are at risk for sabotaging their work.

A high level of anxiety and depression accompanies the common academic problem of inability to complete a Ph.D. dissertation, but one may legitimately ask whether this difficulty is strictly a mental health problem. Students struggling with such difficulties seek help from a variety of sources, including mental health services. Many "writing blocks" have emotional roots; exploring the problem with a therapist may be helpful. Completing a dissertation means different things to different individuals. To some it represents exposing the entire "self" as their worth as a person is bound up in the results. For others it represents risking approval or disapproval by a parental figure–the actual parent or the mentor as a symbolic parent (Nelson, 1961). Students may be as frightened of success as of failure, and they may feel guilt about surpassing someone–a mentor, a sibling or a parent. For others, finishing the dissertation may mean the end of their student status and having to face an uncertain future. Clinical experience in student health services clearly suggests that, while no panacea, individual therapy or participation in groups that focus specifically on the experience of writing a dissertation provide support, understanding and help while students struggle with completing this last requirement for their degree.

Performing arts students in music, voice, drama or dance struggle with putting themselves on display, which is even more stressful when one is being evaluated. Students must be able to ignore "stage fright," formally referred to as performance anxiety or social phobia, and develop the ability to hear negative criticism without feeling personally injured, concerns heightened in graduate school because success in school is a necessary step to earning a living in the arts, an uncertain future even for individuals with great talent.

The graduate school of art and design provides other of challenges. The work is by definition creative and personal for the student, so the judging faculty should be sensitive to the fact that discouragement only increases the difficulty of being creative. If the school atmosphere is not encouraging, doing the expected work will be arduous. Design schools tend to expect a great deal in terms of quantity, to say nothing of quality of work. Sleep deprivation is virtually universal at times. Architecture students must pass their final project review, which is ostensibly a constructive process, but is notorious for being harshly critical.

The fact that the curriculum is inevitably linked to the grading system poses particular problems in the arts. A student completes a project on an assigned problem, puts the finished work on display, and tries to explain and defend it before a committee of individuals actually called "critics." The experience is designed to enhance learning and future creativity and has the potential to be encouraging and supportive. Often this process works well, but it can be upsetting and destructive if the committee–for whatever reason–primarily finds fault. The public setting with classmates and others present can be humiliating and discouraging. Students, after all, are discovering whether or not they are talented enough to make it in a competitive profession. Students may find such exposure devastating to their self-esteem even when intellectually they understand its justification.

In addition to problems that affect all graduate students, some problems specific to particular programs and pressure points within programs are important to acknowledge. Particular stressors may explain why students display more symptoms at certain times during the academic year. Students in law school, for example, have difficult exams at the end of the first semester which establish their class rank, offer recognition by acceptance to "Law Review," and challenge their self-perception as compared to their classmates. During that same first year law students struggle with acquiring a legalistic way of thinking that many fear will hamper their ability to establish intimate relationships.

Medical students take National Board exams at the end of the second year and start their clinical rotations at the same time, a potentially anxiety-producing situation (Bojar, 1961). Business school students often develop self-deprecatory feelings as soon as they enroll. They question their worth and worry about the high toll that will be exacted from them personally adjusting to life in the corporate world (Babcock, 1961; Celis, 1993). Some business schools offer special courses for students and spouses to help them anticipate and prepare for pitfalls of the corporate environment. Business school students also find it difficult to balance the assigned group exercises demanding teamwork with the concurrent intense competition for summer jobs and starting offers.

Divinity school students worry whether they can conduct their own private lives in a manner worthy of the calling of pastor to a congregation. They may also be required to write a statement describing the basis of their personal faith, a daunting project often accompanied by anxiety and uncertainty.

Chapter 10:

Transition from Graduate School

Completion of a graduate program and receipt of the degree are, of course, happy events enthusiastically greeted that dissipate large amounts of anxiety associated with finishing papers, passing final examinations, and negotiating final creative projects. The prospect, however, of leaving the protected environment of school can be accompanied by considerable trepidation. The final year can be spent in attempting to find an appropriate job; the success or failure of this quest will greatly affect the student's mental state. If a satisfactory job has been found and accepted, there are the arduous practical aspects of moving, which may be strenuous but which probably have no great adverse emotional consequences. On the other hand, if the job search is unsuccessful, the future may look bleak and the immediate alternatives grim indeed.

Furthermore, conflicting career opportunities–or lack of them–may necessitate inconvenient arrangements that place considerable stress on students who are in a serious relationship or are married. The competition that is an integral part of graduate school does not disappear at graduation because comparisons still occur about the relative desirability of jobs obtained, clerkships received and projected salaries. These harbingers of ultimate career success are well known, but one needs secure self-esteem not to be negatively affected by them when comparisons are being made. In other words the transition out of graduate school can be just as difficult as other life transitions.

Here, too, the university can play a role in helping the student move out of graduate school just as they assisted in the transition into graduate school. Career counseling is especially meaningful to graduate students as they ap-

[Haworth co-indexing entry note]: "Chapter 10: Transition from Graduate School." Co-published simultaneously in *Journal of College Student Psychotherapy* (The Haworth Press, Inc.) Vol. 14, No. 2, 1999, pp. 87-88; and: *Helping Students Adapt to Graduate School: Making the Grade* (Committee on the College Student, Group for the Advancement of Psychiatry) The Haworth Press, Inc., 2000, pp. 87-88. Single or multiple copies of this article are available for a fee from The Haworth Document Delivery Service [1-800-342-9678, 9:00 a.m. - 5:00 p.m. (EST). E-mail address: getinfo@haworthpressinc.com].

proach the end of their academic experience. Information about opportunities for postgraduate fellowships, clerkships, and licensing examinations are essential for the student. International students will need special help if they are returning to their country of origin or if they have decided to remain in the U.S. The role of the advisor in providing support becomes especially important at this phase of the student's career in the university.

Chapter 11:
Summary

This report about graduate students addresses the interaction of their internal psychological landscape with the external characteristics of the graduate school environment. Graduate students are as diverse in age, interests, prior life experience and geographic origins as graduate programs are diverse in length, structure, size, admission policies, academic requirements and support systems.

The diversity of graduate students has increased as the graduate student population has become more multicultural. International students now represent a growing proportion of the graduate students in American universities. Their problems are complex, and this report calls attention to the importance of recognizing the special needs of this student population.

Prior to this report, little has been written about the developmental, psychological, and emotional complexity of the lives of graduate students compared to undergraduate students. Distress among undergraduates tends to be more visible, immediate, and noisy. This report describes some of the psychological risks inherent in graduate student study as well. Graduate students are a vulnerable population important to the future of our society and very much at risk now that the availability of psychiatric services on campuses is shrinking.

It must be remembered that graduate students are often isolated and receive considerably less support from the university than undergraduate students. While it is important to recognize their status as adults, this should not be used to justify failure to provide them with structure, resources, and a sense of community–all essential to the maintenance of mental health. Their student status strongly challenges their ability to sustain their continued developmental growth from late adolescence to adulthood, an observation that should be remembered by all who interact with them–deans, faculty members and therapists.

[Haworth co-indexing entry note]: "Chapter 11: Summary." Co-published simultaneously in *Journal of College Student Psychotherapy* (The Haworth Press, Inc.) Vol. 14, No. 2, 1999, pp. 89-91; and: *Helping Students Adapt to Graduate School: Making the Grade* (Committee on the College Student, Group for the Advancement of Psychiatry) The Haworth Press, Inc., 2000, pp. 89-91. Single or multiple copies of this article are available for a fee from The Haworth Document Delivery Service [1-800-342-9678, 9:00 a.m. - 5:00 p.m. (EST). E-mail address: getinfo@haworthpressinc.com].

Universities can enhance the academic performance of graduate students by contributing to the quality of life of students through facilitating their sense of belonging and by providing appropriate support to students' sense of worth. A dean of student affairs can offer direct help to graduate students as well as to various graduate and administrative departments. Such help can begin prior to students arriving through pre-admission mailings and through orientation programs which provide appropriate information about the university. Universities can assist in the adjustment of graduate students directly as well as indirectly by providing support and resources for individual graduate departments, teachers and advisors who deal with students. Ongoing support to graduate students can be offered through an office of student affairs to help students relate to one another and with faculty through provision of space and structured activities. Information about housing, financial help, counseling, career planning, fellowships and other important aspects of students' lives need to be made easily available. Graduate students also need help in the transition out of school to the world-at-large through supportive relationships with advisors, counselors and job placement staff.

This report advocates providing psychiatric services for graduate students to address their complex developmental and psychological needs. Administrators often fail to appreciate the importance of psychiatric services which need to be accessible and available year around. Such services are best provided through a student health service located on campus. Budget restrictions may provide short-term savings but have long-term hidden costs. A student who withdraws in the middle of a program is a tangible loss to the university. Universities must ensure that graduate school students not only have adequate health insurance but also that health care is actually available to them. Administrators need to be aware that students may be covered by health insurance but not have access to care because their home state health maintenance organization (HMO) or provider will not cover services in the university community.

Mental health services for graduate students should be provided by persons who are professionally trained and competent. Such services are best provided within an integrated resource consisting of professionals from the psychiatric, psychological, social work, and nursing fields. A range of levels of care should be available, including supportive as well as long-term psychotherapy, medication, and other therapies. Ready access to hospitalization, if needed, should also be available. Treatment plans should be based on competent psychiatric evaluations and diagnoses which include an understanding of the complex interplay between biological, environmental, and psychological factors.

Psychiatric services not only help individuals but also contribute to the community. Graduate students occupy a critical role as teachers within the university and often are in the front lines in dealing with problems of undergraduates. If graduate students are dysfunctional, they will have a far-reaching effect on others as well. Since they are an important resource for faculty and serve as research and teaching assistants, it is therefore in the university's overall self interest to provide care for this important population on campus. Graduate students assume multiple roles not only within the university but also within society as husbands, wives, parents, and teachers. They have a life outside the classroom, library or laboratory. Graduate students represent leaders of the next generation so that a failure to provide them with adequate resources for their support may result in a tragic loss for our society as a whole.

Appendix:

Review of the Literature

There have been few attempts in the literature to address mental health problems specifically in the graduate and professional student population. Generally, studies survey combined populations of undergraduates and graduate students so that it is difficult to estimate the actual prevalence and incidence of emotional problems in graduate student populations. Furthermore, most information is extrapolated from studying students who use the campus mental health services rather than total student populations, and there are many students with problems who choose not to seek help, or at least not at a campus facility.

A survey of Columbia University students is an exception (Bertocci et al., 1992). It attempted to bypass the biases of studying only patient populations by questioning students from all groups about their major areas of concern. In this study roughly two-thirds of the sample were graduate students. The results indicated that academic and school-related concerns were a priority as well as relationship issues and psychiatric problems. There appeared to be certain sub-groups of students who were especially vulnerable and most likely to have significant concerns. These included Asians, self-identified heavy drinkers, undergraduates, and those self-identified as having eating problems and an increased number of physical complaints. Unfortunately, there was no follow-up to determine rates of referral for mental health services or outcomes. This survey broke new ground: most previous studies focused on undergraduates, and, therefore, could not consider differences between graduate and undergraduate students. The Columbia study found that, compared with students in the graduate and professional schools, Columbia undergraduates were statistically more likely to mention concerns about academic matters, love relationships, drug and alcohol use, eating and

[Haworth co-indexing entry note]: "Appendix: Review of the Literature." Co-published simultaneously in *Journal of College Student Psychotherapy* (The Haworth Press, Inc.) Vol. 14, No. 2, 1999, pp. 93-96; and: *Helping Students Adapt to Graduate School: Making the Grade* (Committee on the College Student, Group for the Advancement of Psychiatry) The Haworth Press, Inc., 2000, pp. 93-96. Single or multiple copies of this article are available for a fee from The Haworth Document Delivery Service [1-800-342-9678, 9:00 a.m. - 5:00 p.m. (EST). E-mail address: getinfo@haworthpressinc.com].

weight problems, and anxiety, phobias, and panic attacks. Doctoral students' academic concerns almost always involved "dissertation block."

Each set of graduate students tends to have its own set of stresses. In preparing this report it was decided not to try to document problems in each field, rather to select one as a specimen example. Without question medical students have been the focus of most studies, perhaps because of the feared consequences of impairment in physicians, but also because such students are available and relatively willing to volunteer as subjects. A computer search using the words "medical students" and "stress" as keys unearthed a variety of articles that can be grouped into three main types of study: (1) biological research aimed at uncovering biological changes accompanying stress (Armeria et al., 1996; Carstensen et al., 1994; Dunbar et al., 1993; Iny et al., 1993; Iny et al., 1994; Malarkey et al., 1995; Rospenda et al., 1994; Whitehouse et al., 1996); (2) studies using self-report and scale techniques that focus on strategies designed to cope with stress as well as studies to identify particular periods of increased stress (Deary, 1994; Foster-Williams et al., 1996; Michie et al., 1994; Mosley et al., 1994; Rathbun, 1995; Rodolfa et al., 1995; Stern et al., 1993; Stewart et al., 1995; Wolf, 1994); and (3) individual studies of particular groups and problems (Ackerman et al., 1994; Amato, 1992; Baldwin et al., 1991; Clark et al., 1987, 1988, 1989; Conrad et al., 1989; Flaherty et al., 1993; Guthrie et al., 1995; McAuliffe et al., 1984; Pepitone-Arreola-Rockwell et al., 1991; Plaut et al., 1990, 1993; Rochford et al., 1977; Sacks et al., 1980; Slaby et al., 1972; Westermeyer, 1988; Zoccolillo et al., 1988). Some recent studies have identified the needs of newly recognized groups of medical students: homosexual students (Townsend et al., 1991), married students and those with children (Plaut et al., 1990). Most investigators, however, address the concerns of all medical student populations together, and focus on those students who present for treatment.

Golinger et al. (1991) reviewed the presenting complaints of 100 consecutive medical students between 1984 and 1988. Of these 61% reported relationship problems, 47% family problems and 45% academic problems. Only 7% reported school problems alone as a major concern, a finding that is probably at odds with the Columbia survey cited above (Bertocci et al., 1992). Of note, 92% met DSM-III criteria for adjustment disorder or affective disorder, again highlighting the importance of accurate diagnosis at the time of presentation. A prospective study of one medical school class over a four-year period revealed that 12% of the class at any one time had moderately high scores on a depression scale, and 25% did so at the end of the second year of medical school, a time of particular stress according to a study done in Hong Kong (Stewart et al., 1995). In general, the depression scores were not correlated with grade point averages, family history, or substance abuse except at the highest end of the scale, making it difficult to identify the students at greatest risk (Clark et al., 1988).

Several investigators (Arnstein, 1986; Hawton et al., 1978, 1995; Meilman et al., 1993 and 1994) explored the subject of suicide and its prevention. An older study examined suicide rates by surveying all 116 U.S. medical schools; it reported rates of suicide from 1974-1981 for men. These were comparable to an age-matched sample from the general public. On the other hand, an earlier article reported higher rates for male medical students compared to the general public (Simon, 1978). Rates for women, however, were three to four times that of the general public.

Meilman et al. (1993) highlighted the need for a campus emergency on-call system to help with prevention. A study at Oxford University by Hawton et al. confirmed that rates of suicide were comparable to the age matched general population but showed an over representation of graduate students in completed suicides (Hawton et al., 1995). Approximately 50% of those students had complaints of depression. Hawton, however, noted that it is difficult to compare and contrast rates from different years and different institutions.

Many studies document the significant and possibly increasing use of substances by medical students. Alcohol appears to remain the most commonly used substance (Ashton et al., 1995; Baldwin et al., 1991; Clark et al., 1987; McAuliffe et al., 1984; Westermeyer et al., 1988). The rates for pathological drinking vary across studies from 18% of students reaching standardized criteria (Clark et al., 1987) to 47% showing potentially abusive patterns of use (Westermeyer et al., 1988). Cocaine and marijuana use is also not infrequent; one study reported that 36% of senior medical students had used cocaine on at least one occasion, while 6% had used it in the last month (Conrad et al., 1989). In another survey 21% of second and third year medical students reported using marijuana (Schwartz et al., 1990). These high rates of use of both legal and illicit substances are especially worrisome as high rates (up to 50%) of adult children of alcoholics and drug abusers have been recognized in medical school populations. A surprising result of another study (Clark et al., 1987) showed that alcohol abusers had better grades in the first year and had overall higher scores on Board examinations. Identifying and treating students with abusive patterns of use may be quite challenging; these students are not necessarily going to be impaired academically during the course of their training.

One large survey questioned undergraduates, deans, and mental health providers to examine their perceptions of the availability of psychological services (Plaut et al., 1993). Although the conclusions were limited by a relatively low response rate, it is interesting that there were significant differences among the three groups in their knowledge of the kinds of services that existed, how one obtained help, and what policies there were to protect confidentiality. In general and understandably, the mental health service providers were more knowledgeable than the students. If these results could be extrapolated to groups of graduate students, it would mean that the visibility of available services could usefully be increased. An attempt at the University of California at Los Angeles (UCLA) to increase confidentiality, affordability, and accessibility of mental health services for medical students resulted in a significant increase in the number of self-referrals with 30% of a given class using the service (Pasnau et al., 1994). Most students presented with complaints of depression and anxiety and required referrals for further evaluation and treatment.

Another innovative approach to the recognition and treatment of psychological problems involved the development of a family physician-counselor program for medical students. One hundred first-year students were paired with 15 physicians who reviewed their histories, genograms, and provided physical exams over a one-year period (Davies et al., 1993). Of the class 35% were identified as having at least one psychosocial problem with 80% of the group identified as adult children of alcoholics, 46% with mental illness, and 11% with alcohol abuse. A significant number were referred for further treatment. Another longitudinal study reported good long-term outcomes (professional development and abstinence) for medical students with substance abuse problems who were referred voluntarily or involuntarily for treatment (Ackerman et al., 1994). Clearly there remain many areas for further investigation. However, one can begin to understand the breadth and depth of problems facing the medical student population as well as the significant impact produced by early recognition and treatment.

References

Ackerman, T.F., & Wall, H.P. (1994). A programme for treating chemically dependent medical students. *Medical Education*, 28: 40-46.

Amato, I. (1992). Profile of a field: chemistry–women have extra hoops to jump through. *Science*, 255: 1372-1374.

American Psychiatric Association Committee on confidentiality (1987). Guidelines on confidentiality. *American Journal of Psychiatry*, 144: 1522-1526.

Armario, A., Marti, O., Molina, T., de Pablo, J., & Valdes, M. (1996). Acute stress markers in humans: Response of plasma glucose, cortisol and prolactin to two examinations differing in the anxiety they provoke. *Psychoneuroendocrinology*, 21(1): 17-24.

Arnstein, R.L. (1986). The place of college health services in the prevention of suicide and affective disorders, Chapter 14 (337-361). In G. Klerman (Ed.) *Suicide and depression among adolescents and young adults*, Washington, D.C.: American Psychiatric Press, Inc.

Arnstein, R.L. (1989). Chronically disturbed students, Chapter 3 (29-47). In P.A. Grayson, & K. Cauley (Eds.) *College Psychotherapy*, New York: The Guilford Press.

Ashton, C.H., & Kamali, F. (1995). Personality, lifestyles, alcohol and drug consumption in a sample of British medical students. *Medical Education*, 29(3): 187-193 May.

Babcock, H.H. (1961). Special problems encountered at the graduate school of business administration, Chapter 12 (201-217). In G.B. Blaine, Jr., & C.C. McArthur (Eds.) *Emotional problems of the student*, New York: Appleton-Century-Crofts.

Baldwin, D., Hughes, P., Conard, S. et al. (1991). Substance use among senior medical students: A survey of 23 medical students. *Journal of the American Medical Association*, 265: 2074-2078.

Barinaga, M. (1992). Profile of a field: neuroscience–the pipeline is leaking. *Science*, 255: 1966-1968.

[Haworth co-indexing entry note]: "References." Co-published simultaneously in *Journal of College Student Psychotherapy* (The Haworth Press, Inc.) Vol. 14, No. 2, 1999, pp. 97-104; and: *Helping Students Adapt to Graduate School: Making the Grade* (Committee on the College Student, Group for the Advancement of Psychiatry) The Haworth Press, Inc., 2000, pp. 97-104. Single or multiple copies of this article are available for a fee from The Haworth Document Delivery Service [1-800-342-9678, 9:00 a.m. - 5:00 p.m. (EST). E-mail address: getinfo@haworthpressinc.com].

Benditt, J. (1992). Women in science–pieces of a puzzle. *Science*, 255: 1365.

Benditt, J. (1992). Women in science: The response–letters to the editor. *Science*, 256: 1610-1616.

Bertocci, D., Hirsch, E., Sommer, W., & Williams, A. (1992). Student mental health needs: Survey results and implications for service. *Journal of American College Health*, 41: 3-11.

Blaine, G.B., Jr., & McArthur, C.C. (1961). *Emotional problems of the student*. New York: Appleton-Century-Crofts.

Blos, P. (1967). The second individuation process of adolescence. *Psychoanalytic Study of the Child*, 22: 162-186.

Bojar, S.A. (1961). Psychiatric problems of medical students, Chapter 13 (217-232). In G.B. Blaine, Jr., & C.C. McArthur (Eds.) *Emotional problems of the student*, New York: Appleton-Century-Crofts.

Carstensen, E., & Yudkin, J.S. (1994). Platelet catecholamine concentrations after short-term stress in normal subjects. *Clinical Science*, 86(1): 35-41.

Celis, W. (1993) Business schools hit hard times amid doubt over value of M.B.A. *The New York Times,* Education Section, May 12, 1993, B6.

Clark, D.C., Eckenfels, E.J., Daugherty, S.R., & Fawcett, J. (1987). Alcohol-use patterns through medical school: A longitudinal study of one class. *Journal of the American Medical Association*, 257: 2921-2931.

Clark, D.C., Gibbons, R.D., Daugherty, S.R., & Silverman, C.M. (1987). Model for quantifying the drug involvement of medical students. *International Journal of the Addictions*, 22: 249-271.

Clark, D.C., & Zeldow, P.B. (1988). Vicissitudes of depressed mood during four years of medical school. *Journal of the American Medical Association*, 260: 2521-2528.

Conard, S., Hughes, P., DeWitt, C. et al. Cocaine use by senior medical students. *American Journal of Psychiatry*, 146: 382-383.

Cross, W.E., Jr. (1985). Black identity: Rediscovering the distinction between personal identity and reference group orientation (152-172). In M.B. Spencer, G.K. Brookins, & W.R. Allen (Eds.) *Beginnings: The social and affective development of black children*, Hillside, NJ: Lawrence Erlbaum.

Cross, W.E., Jr. (1995). In search of blackness and Afrocentricity: The psychology of black identity change, Chapter 3 (53-72). In H.W. Harris, H.C. Blue, & E.E.H. Griffith (Eds.) *Racial and ethnic identity: Psychological development and creative expression*, New York: Routledge Publications.

Davies, S., Rutledge, C., & Davies, T. (1993). A family physician-counselor program for medical students. *Family Medicine*, 25: 327-330.

Deary, I. (1994). Need medical education be stressful? *Medical Education*, 28: 55-57.

Dunbar, P.R., Hill, J., & Neale, T.J. (1993). Urinary neopterin quantification indicates altered cell-mediated immunity in healthy subjects under psychological stress. *Australian & New Zealand Journal of Psychiatry*, 27(3): 495-501.

Erikson, E.H. (1968). *Identity youth and crisis.* New York: W.W. Norton.

Erikson, E.H. (1950). *Childhood and society.* New York: W.W. Norton.

Farnsworth, D.L. (1957). Development of college mental health programs (162-189). In D.L. Farnsworth (Ed.) *Mental health in college and university*, Cambridge: Harvard University Press.

Flaherty, J.A., & Richman, J.A. (1993). Substance use and addiction among medical students, residents, and physicians. *Psychiatric Clinics of North America*, 16(1): 189-197.

Foster-Williams, K., Thomas, P., Gordon, A., & Williams-Brown, S. (Eds.) (1996). An assessment of stress among clinical medical students of the University of West Indies. *West Indian Medical Journal*, 45(2): 51-55.

Fry, C.C., & Rostow, E.G. (1942). *Mental health in college.* New York: Commonwealth Fund.

Gibbons, A. (1992). Key issue: Mentoring. *Science*, 255: 1368-1369.

Gibbons, A. (1992). Key issue: Two-career science marriage. *Science*, 255: 1380-1382.

Gibbons, A. (1992). Key issue: Tenure. *Science*, 255: 1386-1389.

Gilligan, C. (1982). *In a different voice: Psychological theory and women's development.* Cambridge, MA: Harvard University Press.

Gold, A.R. (1978). Reexamining barriers to women's career development. *American Journal of Orthopsychiatry*, 48: 690-703.

Golinger, R. (1991). Reasons that medical students seek psychiatric assistance. *Academic Medicine*, 66: 121-122.

Grayson, P.A., & Cauley, K. (Eds.) (1989). *College psychotherapy.* New York: Guilford Press.

Group for Advancement of Psychiatry, Committee on the College Student. *Sex and the college student.* Report 60 (1965). New York: Group for the Advancement of Psychiatry.

Group for the Advancement of Psychiatry, Committee on the College Student. *The educated woman: Prospects and problems.* Report 92 (1975). New York: Mental Health Materials Center.

Group for the Advancement of Psychiatry, Committee on the College Student. *Friends and lovers in the college years.* Report 115 (1983). New York: Mental Health Materials Center.

Group for the Advancement of Psychiatry, Committee on the College Student. *Psychotherapy with college students.* Report 130 (1990). New York: Brunner/Mazel, Inc.

Guthrie, E.A., Black, D., Shaw, C.M., Hamilton, J., Creed, F.H., & Tomenson, B. (1995). Embarking upon a medical career: Psychological morbidity in first year of medical students. *Medical Education*, 29(5): 33-41.

Hartmann, H. (1958). *Ego psychology and the problem of adaptation*. New York: International Universities Press.

Hawton, K., Crowle, J., Simkin, S. et al. (1978). Attempted suicide and suicide among Oxford University students. *British Journal of Psychiatry*, 132: 506-509.

Hawton, K., Simkin, S., Fagg, J. et al. (1995). Suicide in Oxford University students, 1976-1990. *British Journal of Psychiatry*, 166: 44-50.

Healy, B. (1992). Women in science: From panes to ceilings. *Science*, 255: 1333.

Hirschfeld, R.M., & Schatzberg, A.F. (1994). Long-term management of depression. *American Journal of Medicine*, 97: 33S-38S.

Iny, L.J., Suranyi-Cadotte, B.E., Bernier, B., Luthe, L., & Meaney, M.J. (1993). Relationship of social support to [^{3}H] imipramine binding during and after examination stress. *Journal of Psychiatry & Neuroscience*, 18: 143-147.

Iny, L.J., Pecknold, J., Suranyi-Cadotte, B.E., Bernier, B., Luthe, L., Nair, N.P., & Meaney, M.J. (1994). Studies of a neurochemical link between depression, anxiety, and stress from [^{3}H] imipramine and [^{3}H] paroxetine binding on human platelets. *Biological Psychiatry*, 36: 281-291.

Johnson, E.A., & Schwartz, A.J. (1989). Returning students, Chapter 16 (316-334). In P.A. Grayson, & K. Cauley (Eds.) *College psychotherapy*, New York: Guilford Press.

Karasu, T.B. (1990). Toward a clinical model of psychotherapy for depression, II–an integrative and selective treatment approach. *American Journal of Psychiatry*, 147: 269-278.

Liptzin, M.B. (1994). Personal communication.

Malarkey, W.B., Pearl, D.K., Demers, L.M., Kiecolt-Glaser, J.K., & Glaser, R. (1995). Influence of academic stress and season on 24-hour mean concentrations of ACTH, cortisol, and beta-endorphin. *Psychoneuronendocrinology*, 20(5): 499-508.

Martinez, A.M., Huang, K.H.C., Johnson, S.D., Jr., & Edwards, S., Jr. (1989). Ethnic and international students, Chapter 15 (298-316). In P.A. Grayson, & K. Cauley (Eds.) *College psychotherapy*, New York: Guilford Press.

McAuliffe, W. (1984). Non-therapeutic opiate addiction in health professionals: A new form of impairment. *American Journal of Drug and Alcohol Abuse*, 10: 11-22.

McAuliffe, W., Rohman, M., Fishman, P. et al. (1984). Psychoactive drug use by young and future physicians. *Journal of Health and Social Behavior*, 25: 34-54.

McAuliffe, W., Rohman, M., & Wechsler, H. (1984). Alcohol, substance abuse and risk factors of impairment in a sample of physicians-in-training. *Advances in Alcohol and Substance Abuse*, 42: 67-87.

Meilman, P., Hacker, D., & Kraus-Zeilmann, D. (1993). Use of the mental health on-call system on a university campus. *Journal of American College Health*, 42: 105-109.

Meilman, P., Pattis, J.A., & Kraus-Zeilmann (1994). Suicide attempts and threats on one college campus: Policy and practice. *Journal of American College Health*, 42: 147-154.

Menand, L. (1996a). How to make a Ph.D. matter. *The New York Times,* Section 6, September 22, 78-82.

Menand, L. (1996b). How to make a Ph.D. matter. *The New York Times,* Section 6, October 27, 18.

Michie, S., & Sandhu, S. (1994). Stress management for clinical medical students. *Medical Education*, 28: 528-533.

Miller, I.W., & Keitner, G.I. (1996). Combined medication and psychotherapy in the treatment of chronic mood disorders. *Psychiatric Clinics of North America*, 19: 151-171.

Miller, J.B. (1976). *Toward a new psychology of women*. Boston: Beacon Press.

Moran, M. (1992). Mentoring reaps many benefits for mentors, mentees, and profession. *Psychiatric News*, Vol. 27, No. 13, July 3, 16.

Mosley, T.H., Jr., Perrin, S.G., Neral, S.M., Dubbert, P.M., Grothes, C.A., & Pinto, B.M. (1994). Stress, coping, and well-being among third-year medical students. *Academic Medicine*, 69: 765-767.

Nelson, R.L. (1961). Special problems of graduate students in the School of Arts and Sciences, Chapter 11 (186-201). In G.B. Blaine, Jr., & C.C. McArthur (Eds.) *Emotional problems of the student*, New York: Appleton-Century-Crofts.

Neugarten, B.L. (1979). Time, age, and the life cycle. *American Journal of Psychiatry*, 136: 887-894

Notman, M.T., Klein, R., Jordan, J.V., & Zilbach, J.J. (1991). Women's unique developmental issues across the life cycle, Chapter 26. In A. Tasman, & A. Goldfinger (Eds.) *Review of Psychiatry Vol. #10*, Washington, D.C.: American Psychiatric Press, Inc.

Offer, D., & Sabshin, M. (Eds.) (1984). *Normality and the life cycle*. New York: Basic Books.

Pasnau, R., & Stoessel, P. (1994). Mental health service for medical students. *Medical Education*, 28: 33-39.

Paykel, E.S. (1995). Psychotherapy, medication combinations, and compliance. *Journal of Clinical Psychiatry*, 56, supplement 1: 24-30.

Pepitone-Arreola-Rockwell, F., & Core, N. (1991). Fifty-two medical student suicides. *American Journal of Psychiatry*, 138: 198-201.

Pervin, L.A. (1966). The later academic, vocational, and personal success of college dropouts. In L.A. Pervin, L.E. Reik, & W. Dalrymple (Eds.) *The college dropout and the utilization of talent*, Princeton, NJ: Princeton University Press.

Pinderhughes, E. (1989) Biracial identity–asset or handicap? Chapter 4 (73-95). In H.W. Harris, H.C. Blue, & E.H.H. Griffith (Eds.) *Racial and ethnic identity: Psychological development and creative expression*, New York: Routledge Publications.

Pinkerton, R., & Rockwell, K. (1994). Very brief psychological interventions with university students. *Journal of American College Health*, 42: 156-162.

Plaut, S. (1990). Institutional resources for medical students in committed relationships. *Academic Medicine*, 65: 593-599.

Plaut, S., Maxwell, S., Seng, L. et al. (1993). Mental health services for medical students: perceptions of students affairs deans and mental health providers. *Academic Medicine*, 68: 360-365.

Rathbun, J. (1995). Helping medical students develop lifelong strategies to cope with stress. *Academic Medicine*, 70: 955-956.

Reifler, C.B. (1988). Student health: an international interchange. *Journal of American College Health*, 36: 303-305.

Rockford, J., Grant, I., & LaVigne, G. (1997). Medical students and drugs: further neuropsychological and use pattern considerations. *International Journal of the Addictions*, 12: 1057-1065.

Rodolfa, E., Chavoor, S., & Velasquez, J. (1995). Counseling services at the University of California, Davis: helping medical students cope. *Journal of the American Medical Association*, 274: 1396-1397.

Rospenda, K.M., Halpert, J., & Richman, J.A. (1994). Effects of social support on medical students' performances. *Academic Medicine*, 69: 496-500.

Schafer, R. (1966). Talent as danger: psychoanalytic observations on academic difficulty (207-223). In L.A. Pervin, L.E. Reik, & W. Dalrymple (Eds.) *The college dropout and the utilization of talent*, Princeton, NJ: Princeton University Press.

Schwartz, R., Lewis, D., Hoffman, N. et al. (1990). Cocaine and marijuana use by medical students before and during medical school. *Archives of Internal Medicine*, 150: 883-886.

Selvin, P. (1992). Profile of a field: Mathematics–heroism is still the norm. *Science*, Vol. 255 13 March, 1382-1384.

Settlage, C.F., Curtis, J. et al. Conceptualizing adult development. *Journal of the American Psychoanalytic Association*, 36: 347-370.

Silverman, M.M. (1993). Campus student suicide rates: Fact or artifact? *Suicide and Life-threatening Behavior*, Vol. 23, No. 4, Winter, 329-342.

Simon, H. (1978). Mortality among medical students, 1947-1967. *Journal of Medical Education*, 43: 1175-1182.

Slaby, A., Lieb, J., & Schwartz, A.S. (1972). Comparative study of the psychosocial correlates of drug use among medical and law students. *Journal of Medical Education*, 47: 717-723.

Slotnick, H.B., Pelton, M.H., Fuller, M.L., & Tabor, L. (1993). *Adult learners on campus*. Washington, D.C.: The Falmer Press.

Smith, D.G. (1995). Graduate students' health insurance status and preferences. *Journal of American College Health*, 43: 163-168.

Snyder, B.R. (1971). *The hidden curriculum*. New York: Random House-Knopf.

Stern, M., Norman, S., & Komm, C. (1993). Medical students' differential use of coping strategies as a function of stressor type, year of training and gender. *Behavioral Medicine*, 18: 173-180.

Stewart, S.M., Betson., C., Marshall, I., Wong, C.M., Lee, P.W., & Lam, T.H. (1995). Stress and vulnerability in medical students. *Medical Education*, 29: 119-127.

Thase, M.E., Greenhouse, J.B., Frank, E. et al. (1997). Treatment of major depression with psychotherapy or psychotherapy-pharmacotherapy combinations. *Archives of General Psychiatry*, 54: 1009-1015.

Townsend, M., Wallick, M., & Cambre, K. (1991). Support services for homosexual students at US medical schools. *Academic Medicine*, 66: 361-363.

VandeCreek, L., & Knapp, S. (1983). *Tarasoff and beyond: Legal and clinical considerations in the treatment of life-endangering patients*. Sarasota, Florida: Professional Resource Press.

Weissman, M.M., Klerman, G.L., Rounseville, B., & Chevron, E.S. (1995). Interpersonal psychotherapy for depression. *Journal of Psychotherapy Practice and Research*, 4: 340-352.

West, C. (1993). The new cultural politics of difference (3-32). In *Keeping faith: philosophy and race in America*, New York: Routledge Publications.

Westermeyer, J. (1988). Substance abuse among medical trainees: Current problems and evolving resources. *American Journal of Drug and Alcohol Abuse*, 14(3): 393-404.

Whitaker, L.C., & Slimak, R.E. (Eds.) (1990). *College student suicide*. Binghamton, N.Y.: The Haworth Press, Inc. Also published as a special double issue of *The Journal of College Student Psychotherapy* simultaneously Volume 4, No. 3/4, 1990.

Whitehouse, W.G., Dinges, D.F., Orne, E.C., Keller, S.E., Bates, B.L., Bauer, N.K., Morahan, P., Haupt, B.A., Carlin, M.M., Bloom, P.B., Zaugg, L., &

Orne, M.T. (1996). Psychosocial and immune effects of self-hypnosis training for stress management throughout the first semester of medical school. *Psychosomatic Medicine*, 58: 249-263.

Wittenberg, R. (1968). *Postadolescence*. New York: Grune & Stratton.

Wolf, T.M. (1994). Stress, coping and health: Enhancing well-being during medical school. *Medical Education*, 28: 8-17, discussion 55-57.

Zoccolillo, M., Murphy, G., & Wetzel, R. (1986). Depression among medical students. *Journal of Affective Disorders*, 11: 91-96.

Index

Abuse
    alcohol, in graduate students, 75
    in faculty-student relationships, 42
    substance, in graduate students, 75
Academic politics, in graduate school, 39
Academic progress reviews, for graduate students, 17
Advisor(s), for graduate students, 17
Age, "normative," factors contributing to, 22
Alcohol abuse, in graduate students, 75
Alienation, among graduate students, 66
All but dissertation (ABD), of graduate students, 83-85
Anxiety
    affecting completion of degrees, 84
    financial issues and, 49
    in graduate students, 71
    "spotlight," among minority students, 64
Arnstein, R.L., xvi
Attention deficit disorders (ADDs), in graduate students, 71
Autonomy, of graduate students, 23-24

Bipolar disorders, in graduate students, 73-74
Blue, H., xvii
Business school students, degree vs. not degree, factors influencing, 85

Career
    commitment to, graduate school as means of delaying, 10

future, graduate school as means of delaying, 10
Career counseling, for graduate students, 87-88
Character
    defined, 29
    structure of, stabilization of, of graduate students, 29-33
Collaboration, among graduate students, 39-40
Commercial personal loans, for graduate students, 52
Commitment to career, graduate school as means of delaying, 10
Committee on the College Student, of Group for the Advancement of Psychiatry, report by, xv-xvii,1-104
Competitiveness, in graduate school, 37-38
Confidentiality
    psychiatric illness–related, 74-75
    of treatment for graduate students, 81
Counseling, career, for graduate students, 87-88
Cultural issues, facing international students, 66-67

Day care centers, for children of graduate students, 17-18
Depression
    affecting completion of degrees, 84
    in graduate students
        psychotherapy for, 33
        SSRIs for, 32
Developmental issues
    education and, 22
    identity formation, 27-29

Tarasoff doctrine, 774
Teaching assistant(s) (TAs),
        responsibilities of, 50
Teaching assistantships, for graduate
        students, 49-50
Tutor(s), graduate students as, 50-52

University(ies), role in providing
        support for graduate students,
        13-19

Value(s), personal, 33-34
Vigilante, G., xvii

Whitaker, L., xvi-xvii
Wittenberg, R., 33-34